Fatal Depth

Fatal Depth

Deep Sea Diving, China Fever,
and the Wreck of the Andrea Doria

J O E   H A B E R S T R O H

THE LYONS PRESS
GUILFORD, CONNECTICUT
AN IMPRINT OF THE GLOBE PEQUOT PRESS

FOR ROBERTA ROOST

The Lyons Press is an imprint of The Globe Pequot Press.

Printed in the United States of America

Text design by Casey Shain

1 3 5 7 9 10 8 6 4 2

ISBN 1-59228-304-7 (trade paper)

The Library of Congress has cataloged the hardcover edition as follows:

Haberstroh, Joe.
  Fatal depth: deep-sea diving, China fever, and the wreck of the
Andrea Doria / Joe Haberstroh.
      p. cm.
Includes bibliographical references (p.219).
  ISBN 1-58574-457-3 (hc : alk. paper)
  1. Andrea Doria (Steamship) 2. Scuba diving—Accidents—Atlantic
Coast (U.S.) 3. Shipwrecks—Atlantic Coast (U.S.) I. Title.
  GV838.673.A75 H33 2003
  797.2'3—dc21
                                        2002153389

CONTENTS

Acknowledgments

A writer who tells a story about events he or she has not witnessed necessarily enters into a collaboration with a wide range of people, and I extend my appreciation foremost to all the divers whose names appear here. In particular I thank Dan Crowell, shipper of the *Seeker,* who over the course of years and many interviews was unfailingly courteous and professional.

Under difficult emotional circumstances, those closest to the divers who were killed in accidents at the *Andrea Doria* provided valuable insights and critical information. These people include Richard Roost, Sr., and Roberta Roost; Louis and Susan Sicola; Marisa Gengaro; Karen Moscufo; and Mary Beth Byrne.

This book is based on a series of articles I wrote for *Newsday* that appeared in 1999, and on follow-up coverage in subsequent years. Much appreciation is due to the group of senior editors who supported the original project, including Tony Marro, Bob Brandt, Charlotte Hall and Miriam Pawel. Special thanks to my editor on the project, Alex Martin, whose daily demonstration of the highest professional standards inspired me and helped bring the series to life. Additional thanks to my partners on the series, photographer Michael Ach; news artist Rod Eyer; and the staff of the *Newsday* library. Thanks to Gloria Sandler for her help in the retrieval of photos used here.

I would also like to acknowledge the assistance of Lt. Timothy Dickerson, of the U.S. Coast Guard, Marine Safety Office, New Haven, Connecticut. Thanks also to Richard Lefkowitz, for explanations regarding legal actions.

For checking accuracy of technical and/or historical details, thanks to Capt. Robert Meurn, U.S. Merchant Marine Academy, Kings Point, New York; and Joel Dovenbarger, Director of Medical Services, Divers Alert Network. Thanks also to Dan Orr, of DAN.

I must thank Jonathan McCullough, my editor at the Lyons Press, for his wise guidance and thoughtful suggestions for the manuscript. Thanks also to John Waldman, of the Hudson River Foundation, in New York, who introduced me to Jay.

While this book has my name on the cover, it is also the product of many people who have encouraged me over the past year. Besides my parents, these supporters include old friends Greg Rasa and Alan Prill; and newer ones, including Thomas Maier, Andrew Metz and Steve Wick. For their support, much gratitude and affection is also due Maria Hodermarska and Rebecca T. Moore.

Greatest appreciation is reserved for my wife, Elizabeth Moore, who provided intelligent editing but also, as always, love and understanding.

Fatal Depth

Introduction

I knew my drive to Montauk was almost complete when the familiar two-lane highway lifted with the terrain a few miles west of town, above the crouched coastal forest of holly and black oak. Here, eighty miles east of Manhattan, the twisting geography of Long Island's easternmost point rises suddenly into view, a ragged claw extending into the blue confluence of Block Island Sound and the Atlantic Ocean.

I was on my way to see Dan Crowell, captain of the *Seeker*. Neither of us looked forward to the meeting, which took place on a sunny morning one day in the last week of July 1999.

As a reporter for *Newsday,* the daily newspaper on Long Island, I had written a series of articles that summer on the 1998 deaths of three scuba divers who had each dived from the *Seeker,* the sixty-five-foot charter boat owned by Crowell. The men were all exploring the wreck of the *Andrea Doria,* the stylish Italian passenger ship that sank in 1956 as it approached New York.

Academic archaeologists had little interest in the site. In the 1990s, they were far more intrigued with the ancient wares being lifted from Phoenician trading ships, or the brilliant salvage work under way at the site of the sunken Civil War ironclad, the *Monitor.* Other than navigation experts who had long debated the circumstances surrounding the *Andrea Doria's* sinking, few scholars gave the wreck much thought.

In the world of recreational scuba diving, however, the *Andrea Doria* occupied the highest station. Plates, cups, vases, and other trinkets from the wreck are considered the sport's most coveted trophies. The *Doria,* as the ship is known, lies 250 feet down, so only the most skillful divers can lay claim to these prizes. None of the divers who had died was from Long Island, but Crowell docked the boat at a Montauk marina every summer. This fact was sufficient for the newspaper to examine the lives of the three lost men, as well as the subculture that had developed around the *Seeker* itself. Crowell cooperated and graciously opened doors for me with other divers.

Now, a year later, and just one month after the four-part series had appeared, Crowell had lost two more divers. One man, Christopher Murley, who had died as he was swimming on the surface, was a stranger to Crowell. But the other man, Charles McGurr, was a friend.

McGurr had worked as a crew member on the trip. He had died after he descended to the *Doria* with two other divers, indicated he was aborting the dive, then appeared to begin an ascent. Hours later, Crowell discovered his friend's body wedged into the wreck where he had apparently fallen.

McGurr had decided to give himself the diving trip as a present to himself for his birthday. Making a safe dive on the wreck of the *Andrea Doria* is the ultimate rite of passage in Northeast shipwreck diving. Divers who pull it off have devoted themselves to mastering the most complex scuba diving equipment and techniques known outside the military. The dangers of the depth, the changeable nature of the sea conditions, and the remoteness from emergency medical assistance mean that anyone who undertakes a dive on the *Andrea Doria* is presumed to be competent. These divers are assumed to be able to take care of themselves if something goes wrong.

McGurr had no doubts as to which charter boat would take

him there. The *Seeker's* singular status in the society of ship-wreck divers was based on its divers' uncanny talent at taking more artifacts than anyone else from the wrecks they visited. They were the best diggers. Staying for only fifteen or twenty minutes at a time on the wrecks—that's as long as their air sup-plies generally held out—the divers of the *Seeker* brought back inscribed bells, antique compasses, brass lanterns, and fistfuls of bullets. Divers use all these things to keep score with each other and to overdecorate their dens.

When I arrived at the marina in Montauk, Crowell was vig-orously brushing a greasy stain that marked the boat's waterline from stem to stern. Even after more than four decades, the *Doria* continues to seep oil and oil-based fluids, and any boat that vis-its the site leaves with streaks coloring its hull. After giving me a mock look of horror, he greeted me with a handshake. No, he did not want to talk, but yes, he would. He looked exhausted. His brown eyes were reddened and appeared half closed. He acknowledged that the stress of yet another death, especially that of his friend McGurr, had shaken him.

The passion divers such as Crowell and others have for exploring the wreck of the *Doria* has fascinated me more than any other aspect of the events of the summers of 1998 and 1999, and of the investigations and recriminations that have continued since that time. Why do they do it, and what were the conse-quences, if any, of all that had happened?

I am not a scuba diver, and no one witnessed the deaths of four of the five divers this book discusses, so reconstructing events associated with *Seeker* poses a challenge. To tell the story, I interviewed dozens of scuba divers, and their families and friends, in person and on the telephone. Most were from Long Island and New Jersey. When more than one person has recounted the same event, I reconstructed conversations and scenes on board the *Seeker*. These passages often appear here without attribution. For corroboration, I relied on investigative records of the U.S. Coast Guard, which include written statements supplied by the divers within hours of the accidents, as well as radio logs from the *Seeker*. At some point in the story of each man's difficulty underwater, it is impossible, of course, to know exactly what took place.

To re-create the *Andrea Doria*'s sinking in 1956, to detail early scuba exploration of the site, and to explain rudiments of diving physiology, I relied on personal interviews and written material, including federal court records and previously published works.

The single most important source was always Dan Crowell. For me, he came to embody the sport of technical scuba diving. He swaggered, was often profane, and usually funny. Like the other divers, he was as enthusiastic about diving as children are about ice cream. The thrill they get from breathing underwater is boundless, and the bonds that develop among divers who descend far beyond the informal recreational limit of 130 feet are remarkably intense. Crowell was at the top of the wreck divers' artificial hierarchy, a strange little kingdom where the men (and they are almost all men) earn quasi-military shoulder patches with each new advanced-diving course they pay for and pass, and where rank is based on the number of dives they make on the sunken ships scattered around the Northeast, all within a hundred miles of shore.

At times, Dan Crowell outraged me. He seemed dismissive of people who had trouble mastering the diving skills he had honed, and he spouted glib, fatalistic comments about the men who had been lost. He liked to say that most of the men had died pursuing their dreams. These were dreams whose realization the divers sometimes compared to battlefield victories, and to historical adventures of the first order. Yet they held little societal resonance beyond the self-referential bubble that enclosed the men as they bent elbows in Montauk at the Liar's Saloon.

The sport in most respects thrived outside government oversight. Dan and the other divers of the *Seeker* could do whatever they wanted, and they often did, and they did not care much what outsiders thought of them, and I was fascinated by their king-of-the-hill attitude.

That day at Montauk, Crowell looked beat, and even hurt, maybe, but he had not lost his ironic sense of humor. He wore that as easily as his part-down-the middle haircut, circa 1975, as he showed when a woman on the docks called out to him, "I love your boat!"

"Want to buy it?" he replied.

"Well, how much?" She laughed.

"Cheap!"

Dan Crowell laughed, too. Then he turned again to see if he could wash the dark stain from the white hull of the *Seeker.*

One

Dan Crowell was a human submarine. He shouldered more than two hundred pounds of equipment to sustain him underwater, including air tanks, a weight belt, high-intensity lights, and powerful swim fins, and he moved headfirst with practiced efficiency down the anchor line to the wreck of the *Andrea Doria*.

Daylight briefly lit his descent, in wavering beams, but the white sun shut down fast, in seconds, as if a retractable roof had clicked into place. Divers liked to talk about how they could hear the whir of propellers from passing container ships miles away, but this was not the case as Dan pulled himself hand-over-hand down the line. The only sounds were the hiss as Dan drew cold, compressed air from his air tanks and the rush of bubbles that buzzed upward when he exhaled.

It was June 23, 1998. The visibility in the water was about fifty feet, which was not bad for this wreck site forty-five miles south of Nantucket Island. As he descended, Dan could see only a short section of the line before him. It looped in the darkness like a luminous strand in a spider's web.

About five minutes passed before Dan had descended 180 feet, and the ship's hull came into view below him like a runway in the fog. It was a wide and rusty slope that faded in the blue-green void, an artificial reef troweled everywhere with barnacles and planted with undulating rows of beckoning sea anemones. The expanse was recognizable as a ship's hull only by

7

the encrusted openings that were all that remained of the great ocean liner's portholes. The current there stirred particles of silt and columns of plankton as if they were spinning motes of dust.

Relaxed and well oriented to the wreck he had explored more than a hundred times before, Dan dipped his head and kicked his fins lightly, so he wouldn't dislodge clouds of silt that would obscure his vision. Like a hawk gliding low over a freshly cut field, he passed over the barnacle-encrusted portholes, each perforation a well into blackness. The glass panels had long been absent, due either to the erosion of the steel that surrounded them or to the salvage efforts of enterprising divers such as Dan Crowell.

He swam toward what the divers called Gimbel's Hole. The opening, as big as a double-sized garage door, had been cut almost twenty years earlier by wreck divers led by Peter Gimbel, the department store heir and adventurer. Dan planned to snake around inside the deteriorating ship to a collapsed cabinet that held hundreds of pieces of china that had survived the ship's free fall to the seafloor.

The *Andrea Doria* had four hundred dining tables spread among its nine decks, and it carried different sets of dishes and flatware for first-, cabin-, and tourist-class passengers, along with a set for officers. In the first-class lounge, the staff served cakes and tea and coffee with an exquisite set of hand-painted china that depicted country scenes from ancient Japan. The stewards had more china than they knew what to do with. Sometime the finest pieces held handfuls of matchbooks, or hard candy, or loose cigarettes.

Divers came from around the United States and the world to descend to the ship for these delicate porcelain prizes. Here was the hard proof that they had mastered the peculiar challenges of the *Andrea Doria* wreck site—the strong ocean currents, the danger involved in going inside the ship, the frequently poor visibility, and, most obviously, the extreme depth, well beyond the informal recreational scuba diving limit of 130 feet. For many deep divers, a descent to the *Andrea Doria* marked the pinnacle of their underwater careers. They began to call the wreck their sport's "Mount Everest."

For those who wish to compare climbers' obsession with the world's highest peak to divers' captivation with the *Doria*, the parallels present themselves. Both destinations are remote from sophisticated medical care in case of emergency. Exploration of both the mountain and the wreck requires self-contained breathing equipment (though a minority of climbers ascend Everest without oxygen). The summit experience in Nepal is often brief—just a few minutes to enjoy the view—and a dive on the *Doria* might last for only twenty minutes before a diver has to begin a precisely calculated, ninety-minute ascent to the surface. In the 1990s, an increasing number of adventurers was determined to summit Everest and explore the *Andrea Doria*. In 1993, 129 people made it to the top of Mount Everest, marking the first season in which more than 100 people had achieved the feat. In 1998, 120 people would summit the peak. Similarly, the 1990s brought unheard numbers of divers to the *Andrea Doria*. To explain the trend, most people cited a surge in the culture of extreme sports and a robust U.S. economy. A dive that in the 1980s was reserved for twenty or thirty people per season, which lasted from late June through early August, began to attract more than a hundred every summer, with everyone paying about a thousand dollars for a spot on a dive boat. Finally, just as alpine climbers acknowledge that the allure of their sport is in part derived from their experience of mortal danger, deep divers admit that at least some of their thrill comes from testing the outer limits of physical safety.

It's inadvisable to push the comparison too far, however. The typical member of an Everest expedition is certainly more physically fit than the average *Andrea Doria* diver. Those who assault Everest also work in large teams, whereas divers routinely explore the *Doria* by themselves, in defiance of the buddy-system ethic that rules less advanced forms of the sport. Also, far more people attempt and fail to summit Everest than those who try but fail to dive the *Doria*.

Most of the divers who get out to the *Doria* make successful dives. People such as Dan Crowell think the "Mount Everest" nickname intensely corny and hyped. He knows that *Doria* divers generally self-select and that most people who are there know what they're doing. At the same time, he acknowledges that the wreck draws the best divers or, at least, the braver among them, and that these divers genuinely consider a dive to the *Andrea Doria* as an important lifetime accomplishment.

The danger is real. Seven men had died at the wreck site since 1981. Many divers have seen the stomach-churning photograph of John Ormsby, a Florida diver who drowned on the wreck after his ankle became entangled in a cable. The cable had wrapped around his foot so many times—Ormsby had evidently struggled to free himself but succeeded only in tightening the cable's hold—that the police for a while investigated the death as a homicide. They couldn't believe a diver could get into that much trouble.

Dan knew different. He had wriggled hundreds of feet into the murky labyrinth that was the *Andrea Doria*. On that Tuesday, June 23, 1998, he and one of his crew members on the current trip, Gary Gentile, one of the foremost divers in the Northeast, found the collapsed china cabinet. They had to make a few turns inside the muck-filled wreck to the cabinet, and such maneuvers can be tricky inside a dark, sunken ship. This was a 697-foot passenger liner with large public rooms and wide companionways stacked on each other, but much of it collapsed in unpredictable places every year. Because the wreck is on its side, its walls, or what remained of its walls, were now ceilings or floors, and the divers had to remember which was which, and the current always seemed to be ripping a few more electrical cables loose. These could coil around the airflow knobs on a scuba tank, and divers had to carefully cut themselves free, but such movements could trigger a curtain of silt to descend, and so they stayed patient and waited for that to settle. Finally, gaining access to the blown-open china compartments often demanded a full-extension reach past razor-edged petals of rusted steel.

It was all worth it to get to the china hole. That's what such caches are called in any given diving season. That's why they were all here.

Dan sensed that the china cabinet would be a profitable destination for all the charter customers he would take all summer to the *Andrea Doria* until late August, when the weather offshore began to turn rough and he ended his *Doria* work for the year. Still, he wasn't yet certain he wanted his customers nosing around this find. Not, at least, until he could make the opening more obvious.

He saw no sense getting people excited prematurely. Dan did not like people to get too excited. What Dan called the "greed factor" sometimes led people to make mistakes in the wreck. It made things needlessly complicated. Dan didn't talk a lot about the greed factor, though. He did not like to attribute diving errors to emotions. People just forgot their training sometimes. He thought he might even run a safety line from the ship's hull and down to the cabinet. It wasn't the sort of thing he really believed in or needed himself, but he also knew that very few divers could match his experience on the *Andrea Doria*. Some divers would do just about anything to get a piece of china.

So for a short while, he would keep this china hole quiet. He'd discuss it with Gary Gentile alone. He reached into the hole and gently removed a few saucers from the pile. He swung one of the pieces in front of his mask and, through the red rain of rust he had dislodged with his arm movement, he could see that two gold lines were braided against a maroon band around the saucer's lip. This was first-class china. He nestled the china into a mesh bag knotted to his diving rig. This was a china hole well worth returning to. But for now, up on the *Seeker*, he and Gentile called the cache "Secret Spot No. 26."

Dan was in his element exploring the wreck. Other divers of his rank invariably described him as a natural athlete who moved with efficiency and grace under the sea. He was forty years old. He had been diving for about twenty-five years, ever since he and a friend had borrowed the friend's father's diving gear in National City, California, the scruffy San Diego suburb where he had grown up. He still carried an air of sleepy San Diego. With his hooded brown eyes and boyish bangs, he even looked sleepy. He unfailingly downplayed his diving exploits as "no big deal." Maneuvering inside the wrecks was relatively safe, he liked to say, as long as you had studied the ship's layout, remembered your training, and stayed within your capabilities. Skippering charter trips to the *Andrea Doria* and other diving sites provided only part of his income. He was also a professional diver. He fixed submerged pipes and bridge piers around the New York area, using wrenches as big as baseball bats, and the Coast Guard called on him to retrieve the occasional body from a sunken fishing boat. On the job, he spent hours in the water, his air supplied from the surface and pumped to him in tubes.

As a scuba diver, he had been part of a team that discovered a long-lost World War II German submarine, and that "expedition"—divers were always using that word—had been featured in a television documentary. By 1998, he had also made 120 dives on the *Andrea Doria*. At diving shows where Dan Crowell spoke, he was invariably described as the shipwreck's "master."

Dan and Jennifer Samulski, the thirty-three-year-old New Jersey woman to whom he said he was "eternally engaged," had owned the *Seeker* for three years. Dan had dived off the boat for a few years in the early 1990s, then served as a crew member for the former owner, Bill Nagle.

The *Seeker* enjoyed a rowdy reputation as the best ride to the *Andrea Doria* for the newest generation of deep divers, and it always seemed to bring back the most china. Dan had taken seven charters to the *Andrea Doria* that first summer in 1995. Two years later, they had managed to get ten charters out to the site, with each trip ferrying about a dozen paying customers and four or five crew members. The crew didn't always do what you might expect of a crew member, such as driving the boat or helping the paying divers. Sometimes they just dived on their own and with their presence provided a certain *Seeker* atmosphere. A *Seeker* diver, it was said, didn't seem to think a dive was worth doing unless it went below 150 feet.

Virtually all the divers were men, and the *Seeker* was a floating locker room, with lots of adolescent joshing punctuating the sophisticated shop talk about gas mixing and rebreathers. The crew, Dan Crowell's friends from New Jersey mostly, often seemed to hold themselves apart (though this was natural when they actually were working). At night they often sat around in the *Seeker*'s cabin and watched videos of *The Abyss* and trashed the customers aboard who had traveled from Florida or Michigan for the dives of their lives but who had rigged their tanks, well, in a seriously dumb-ass way, of course, with regulators flopping around very unstreamlined.

Exploring the *Andrea Doria* was what New Jersey diver Bart Malone called "big-boy diving," and so Dan always brought along a few of the big boys. On the June 1998 charter, Dan had Gary Gentile and John Moyer working as crew. Gentile published dive-training manuals and beautifully illustrated guides to various shipwrecks, and he participated in the first salvage surveys of the *Monitor*. Quiet aboard, he would chat with a diver if approached. Mostly, though, he'd be in the *Seeker*'s main cabin, typing. He was constantly sought out by reporters who needed to cite an expert on wrecks, diving safety, even diving physiology, though he seemed to be quoted less frequently when he began to charge a "consulting fee" for interviews.

Moyer was a scholarly diver from southern New Jersey. A biology major in college, he worked in an accounting job with a chain of pharmacies owned by his wife's family. To others, he seemed to have substantial resources with which to pursue just about any line of inquiry about the *Andrea Doria* that piqued his interest. Once, he traveled to Genoa to speak to the *Andrea Doria*'s surviving crew, and he went to federal court to secure salvage rights to some of the larger objects hidden on the sunken ship. He supervised a team of divers to lift several colorful ceramic friezes from the wreck, and kept them stored in a specially built shed in his backyard. He had rigged an underwater vacuum once to suck muck from a *Doria* room he felt certain contained the ship's main bell. He was wrong, but his determination and inventiveness impressed anyone who knew anything about the conditions on the wreck.

By 1998, the *Seeker* crowd had eclipsed the charter boat *Wahoo,* which was based on Long Island. Its barrel-chested owner, Steve Bielenda (known for twenty years as the "King of the Deep," a sobriquet he didn't discourage), had for years been the leader in the *Andrea Doria* charter business. But Bielenda never took the numbers out to the *Doria* that Dan did. In the late 1990s, his captains on the *Wahoo* led two or three charter per summer while Dan scheduled ten. If Bielenda was the entrepreneur who invented the three-day dive charter to the *Andrea Doria*, Dan and Jenn were the ones who marketed the idea, and themselves, and provided an outlet for the numerous new deep divers of the '90s who wanted to test their mettle on the ultimate dive.

Sometimes the divers of the *Seeker* mined the *Andrea Doria* as if it were their private lode of sunken treasure. Once, they had used their valuable dive time to bolt a steel grate on the *Doria's* hull to bar access to a china hole. They even left a sign there: CLOSED FOR INVENTORY—PATRONS AND CREW OF THE *SEEKER*. Dan's divers liked to point out that when they shoved, it was usually because they had been pushed. The skipper of a rival boat, after all, had once shotgunned the *Seeker's* marker buoy at the *Doria*.

The first trip of 1998 had been set for June 22 to June 24. Eighteen people would be aboard; six crew members, including Dan and Samulski, would accompany twelve customers organized by a dive shop near Atlantic City, New Jersey. Their leader was Gene Peterson, who owned the Atlantic Divers shop and who had been teaching people to dive for more than twenty years. A small group of divers had been working with Peterson for several years, adding to their training with him course by course. The *Andrea Doria* trip was their annual highlight.

It was the morning of June 23 when Crowell was sizing up the china hole. Up on the deck of the *Seeker*, he had told Jenn Samulski that he would spend twenty-five minutes on the bottom. She had written that information down on the meticulous chart she kept for every diver. There, she recorded how long the diver planned to be underwater doing his or her dive, the hour and minute an individual diver went in the water, the same for when he or she would come out. Knowing all the times helped Jenn keep track of who was diving and when to expect them back.

The *Seeker's* divers may have had a reputation for pushing the envelope, and for an arrogant attitude toward competing charter outfits, but the operation was also known for professionalism and safety. Invariably, Dan sat everyone down when the boat arrived at the *Andrea Doria* site and reminded them of the conditions at the sunken ship—he or one of the most senior crew members would survey the ship when they dived to set the *Seeker*'s anchor line to a mooring permanently hooked in to the wreck. He urged them all to operate within their capabilities. The ship's sheer size might be disorienting to newcomer divers, he reminded them. If a diver used a porthole to mark the distance from the line leading back up to the *Seeker*, the diver had to keep in mind that there would be hundreds of such portholes. Taking unnecessary risks was stupid, he said. Plan your dive and dive your plan. Yes, it was a hokey cliché of scuba diving, but it made sense, especially on this merciless wreck. More than anything, Dan hated sloppy divers who didn't know how inexperienced they actually were.

He also preferred that the less seasoned people aboard dive as two- or three-man teams. He couldn't quite imagine most of these particular customers, as good as they were, exploring the wreck by themselves. Under the ownership of Dan and Jenn, the *Seeker* had never lost a diver.

Jenn also kept track of what kind of air the divers planned to breathe. Few divers on a *Seeker* charter breathed regular air from their scuba tanks. Instead of breathing air's normal blend of oxygen and nitrogen, they breathed a "Trimix" blend of oxygen, nitrogen, and helium. In doing so, they were the beneficiaries of decades of medical research, much of it conducted for the U.S. Navy. In developing Trimix, the researchers had addressed the phenomena known as oxygen toxicity and nitrogen narcosis, the two chief maladies of deep diving.

Oxygen toxicity, which often triggers convulsions and underwater blackouts, is caused when divers breathe oxygen under pressure.

Nitrogen narcosis results from the toxic effect of nitrogen under high pressure. Its main symptom is a disorientation also known as the "martini effect" because it feels like being drunk. The deeper the diver goes, the more pronounced the effect. Each additional fifty feet feels like drinking another martini on an empty stomach. Jacques Cousteau, with characteristically poetic language, called this physiological phenomenon "the rapture of the deep."

"I am personally quite receptive to nitrogen rapture," Cousteau wrote in *The Silent World*. "I like it and fear it like doom."

Under the spell of nitrogen narcosis, divers have reported they first feel a sense of mild euphoria. But then, their mental processes degrade, become syrupy, and their short-term memory suffers. The effect is temporary, but it can be deadly. The divers' sense of judgment erodes. Most dangerous, they can lose their sense of time, and although scuba diving provides its participants the illusion of weightlessness and of detachment from humdrum reality, it is a sport ruled ruthlessly by the clock. Besides equipment failures and surprise physical problems, it's poor judgment that kills shipwreck divers. Under the spell of nitrogen narcosis, divers are tempted to stay down too long.

By replacing a bit of the oxygen and nitrogen, the helium in Trimix tends to reduce the potential for oxygen toxicity and nitrogen narcosis.

The popularity of Trimix has grown in particular with divers who go to what they call technical depths, below the recreational limit of 130 feet, where nitrogen is more easily is absorbed into their tissues. The physiology is straightforward. For every thirty-three feet in ocean water, the nitrogen gas pressure increases another 14.7 pounds per square inch. As divers drop deeper, the pressure compresses the breathing gas mixture, so it is more quickly absorbed into their bloodstream and tissues. Time is also a variable: The longer divers stay down underwater—"at depth" it is called—the more nitrogen dissolves in their bodies. Divers need ways to reduce their nitrogen intake, and Trimix provides that.

Divers who dive for years using plain air become accustomed to the disorientation they experience, so they learn to exercise conservatism at deep depths because, with every minute they remain, they know they are losing the ability to make good decisions. But this level of skill takes years to master. For many divers, Trimix appeared to level the field. It helped them speedily make the deep dives that the previous generation of divers, who relied only on air, had taken years to achieve.

Suddenly it seemed everyone was a technical diver, their jacket sleeves studded with the patches awarded by the dive-training agencies upon the completion of their courses. The bad ones were called "patch divers." They trained up in a couple of years to attempt the *Andrea Doria*, a feat previously reserved for those who had dived ten years or more.

Trimix also helps divers speed up what may be the only boring aspect of their sport, and that is decompression. Divers must ascend from deep depths slowly, or "decompress." If they ascend too quickly, the nitrogen they have absorbed into their bloodstream and tissues through their lungs—which enters their blood at a higher rate as they descend to greater depths—will not have time to safely pass back from their bloodstream and tissues to their lungs, where it is exhaled.

Decompression forces divers to ascend in prescribed increments. They spend up to several minutes at previously plotted stops to give the nitrogen enough time to safely dissolve and pass back into their bloodstream.

If they go up too fast, however, the nitrogen could enter their system as bubbles, which could result in a debilitating case of decompression sickness, also known as the bends. The nitrogen bubbles can crush blood vessels and tissue from inside and out, and they can form in the veins that return blood to the heart, or be carried along in arteries transferring blood from the heart to other parts of the body. Too many nitrogen bubbles can slow blood flow and hamper motor function by crushing nerves. The bends are painful, and sometimes fatal. Divers can fill their decompression air tanks with Trimix, however, and, by reducing the nitrogen, lower the amount of time they spend decompressing. This raises the chances they can dive more than once on a given day.

Dan Crowell, on his dive on June 23, planned to be in the water ninety-nine minutes, but roughly sixty-eight of these minutes would be spent in decompression, hanging on the anchor line he had earlier used to descend to the ship. He had planned to log twenty-five minutes of "bottom time," the period during which he swam around the ship or inside it. He cut the dive several minutes short that day, though.

For his first decompression stops, Dan breathed a tank that contained a reduced amount of nitrogen; instead of the 79 percent of nitrogen contained in the regular air we breathe, one of his decompression tanks contained only 64 percent nitrogen.

Carrying the different kinds of air on a deep dive means that *Andrea Doria* divers sometimes drop into the water with as many as five tanks clipped to their backs. Each tank has a hose attached and each hose has a regulator, the device that divers use to draw air from the tanks. The complicated rigs, with multiple tanks, hoses, and regulators, start to look like experiments out of horror-movie laboratories, even if the divers tend to compete to see who can achieve the most streamlined package. Dan describes technical wreck diving as "gear intensive." It can be unforgiving. Grabbing the wrong regulator and sucking a few breaths out of it can cause convulsions and death, or maybe just panic, which even if it lasts just a few seconds sometimes prompts divers to make rash decisions.

He came out of the water that day at seven minutes past one, stepping on the diamond-plate panel he had installed on the *Seeker's* gunwales, where the divers hoisted themselves back aboard. He had been in the water for one hour and twenty-four minutes. It was sixty-five degrees. The sky was a porcelain dome of blue. Conditions were perfect. The current moved only half a knot per hour, which meant that the divers could hang on without difficulty to the line that stretched from the *Seeker* down to the wreck. The sun's rays flashed off dozens of scuba tanks lined up along the side of the *Seeker's* deck, in close ranks like little soldiers. A couple of dry suits flapped from the rails, airing out. Dan saw that Gary Gentile was on deck. A signal of mutual understanding traveled between them. They began to discuss Secret Spot No. 26.

Shoulder-to-shoulder, they squinted at the *Andrea Doria* deck plans that had been taped near the door to the main cabin of the *Seeker*.

PLANO DELLE SISTEMAZIONI PASSEGGERI—plan of passenger accommodation—the five-foot-tall poster said at the top. All the *Andrea Doria* passengers were presented a smaller version of these plans, printed on white paper with black ink. In schematic style, they laid out ten of the ship's eleven decks, with icons for each chair, table, bunk, and bidet.

Secret Spot No. 26 was on the ship's Foyer Deck, seventh down from what once was the top deck of the *Andrea Doria*. This was the deck entered through Gimbel's Hole. The hole improved on a smaller cut through which divers in 1964 had dragged the bronze statue of Andrea Doria himself, the famed Italian admiral of the sixteenth century. They used hacksaws to separate the admiral from the ship. The centerpiece of the deck was the oval foyer for first-class passengers. From here, passengers could go aft to the lounge and have a drink, or forward to the chapel and say a prayer.

Gary Gentile had spotted the new china hole first—in what appeared to be a closet that was once behind a door at the bottom of a stairwell.

Gentile and Dan tried to pinpoint the location of the china hole on the ship's plans. The closet seemed to be off the first-class dining room, which was two-thirds of the way back from the ship's bow. From Gimbel's Hole, the closet demanded a long swim—a deep penetration, the divers would say.

Using the old plans, and through repeated dives, divers such as Dan and Gentile had committed to memory whole sections of the *Andrea Doria*'s deck-by-deck maze. With this technique, known as progressive penetration, they were able to return to treasure spots but also keep themselves safe.

The conversations between the two men had not gone unnoticed by Jim Schultz, Paul Whittaker, and Craig Sicola, three divers who were part of Gene Peterson's charter group. They all had links to Long Beach Island, where Craig lived, and had been diving together for a few years. Schultz and Whittaker were making their first dives on the *Andrea Doria*. Schultz, an accountant, had spent almost two thousand dollars for new tanks and regulators for the trip. Whittaker, a former marine, was a state trooper in New Jersey. He had made his first dive on the wreck that morning and had been telling people that entering the ship felt like walking into a darkened gymnasium. Prepared to be crammed into tight-fit companionways, he instead was stunned by the sheer size of the interiors. Whittaker was deeply interested in the history of famous ocean liners, and he had been thrilled during his dive to have swum along the outside of the *Doria*'s long black hull.

Craig immediately noticed the small stack of china Dan had brought up from the wreck. Many aboard had the china patterns committed to memory and had been excited that Dan had emerged with first-class saucers. Craig asked Dan where he got the china.

Dan and Gentile winked at each other and started with the "Secret Spot No. 26" talk. They tried to make a joke out it. No, really, Craig said, where? Craig asked in a loud voice, the result of years working with nail guns in his construction business: "Where is this stuff?" At first, Dan did not answer him directly. Although he would not hesitate at dressing down even a paying customer who risked his life and those of others with crude diving techniques—someone descending on the anchor line, for instance, and unnecessarily jostling other divers hanging on the line during their decompression stops—he didn't exactly want to put Craig in his place. Dan didn't enjoy conflict. Charters were supposed to be fun.

Craig had a poor sense about his relative lack of seasoning on the *Andrea Doria*. He had five dives to the ship. Dan had 120. To a normal recreational diver, perhaps someone who learned the basics while vacationing in the Bahamas and dived in trunks and with a single tank of air, Craig Sicola was an expert. But in the field of *Andrea Doria* diving, he ranked as a beginner. Still, no matter their varying experience levels, the *Andrea Doria* divers were all aggressive to a degree, and Craig persisted that afternoon and into the humid evening. He focused on the senior divers— Dan, Gentile, Bart Malone, Steve Gatto, and John Moyer.

"I want to get some china," he told them.

Dan finally told him not to worry so much, that he was thinking about running a safety line into the china hole. Divers could then follow the line into the ship and back out.

Craig wanted to know the exact location anyway. What stairwell? How far back? Some of the divers began in a joking way to talk about China Fever. This was their diagnosis for Craig. They urged him to regain some perspective, for the sake of his safety and that of anyone who buddied up with him on the next day's dives. For a while, Craig did seem to have gotten the message. Then he started in again on Dan and Moyer. This time, Dan was blunt.

"Look, Craig, you don't have the experience level to go to

this place right now," he said. "Where we went, it's way beyond you. We need to check it out, investigate it more, and we will. At your particular skill level, you don't belong there."

The summer moon soon lifted above the horizon. The *Seeker*'s wooden timbers creaked as it rocked in the short off-shore swell. Yellow arrows of light shot from the main cabin, where a couple of men tinkered with gas-mix formulae on laptop computers. Others dozed on the red vinyl bunks. Craig was on the stern deck with Jenn Samulski and Steve Gatto. The moonlight threw a light like alabaster on the *Andrea Doria* ship plans, and Craig stood and studied them.

Ponte del Sol. Sun Deck.

Craig told Gatto he was offended by Dan and Gentile and their talk of Secret Spot. No. 26. Gentile had been first to use the "secret spot" obfuscation with Craig. Gentile rubbed him wrong, typing away on another book between dives and sharing inside jokes with Dan and Moyer. "Craig, listen. I'll tell you why Gary said that," Gatto said. "It's in a bad spot and stairwells are very disorienting. He doesn't want you to get lost, and it's for your benefit."

Gatto told him about Dan's offer to run the safety line.

"Yeah," Craig said, "but that's not necessarily going to get me china."

Craig had asked a lot of questions that day, and his detective work apparently had led him to believe that a cache of china could be found on the Foyer Deck, in the kitchen. Made sense. He looked again at the plans. *Ponte Passeggiata*. Promenade Deck. Samulski, who was sitting on a white cooler, the kind fishermen used for stowing their catch, spoke up. "Craig, an attitude like that is only going to get you a pine box."

Craig turned to her. He seemed to take in what she'd said. How could he not? Then, quietly, he said, "That would be bad."

Gatto added, "Yes, that would be bad. If you're patient, man, the china will come." With that, Gatto went inside.

Craig remained at the cabin door, near the deck plans. *Ponte Vestiboli.* Foyer Deck. There, inked on the plans, was the familiar oval shape of the first-class foyer, just below where one of the divers had sketched in the garage-door hole cut into the side by previous divers. Farther to the left on the plans, Craig saw what appeared to be a Mondrian grid of unlabeled rooms. The kitchen.

The next day dawned clear and warm. Dan sat in the pilothouse, an airy perch above the *Seeker's* main cabin, and made his daily notation on the weather. He summarized it with a single word: "Calm."

Craig was supposed to go diving with Whittaker and a third diver, Lyn Del Corio. But when the two other men stepped from the *Seeker* and plunged into the water, Craig was not ready. It wasn't like Craig at all. He worked hard and played hard and was always ready. Schultz watched his buddy slowly pull on his gear. Craig was "dragging it out," Schultz said, like a five-year-old putting his clothes on in slow motion before school on a winter morning. Whittaker jumped in at 10:26 A.M., Samulski noted in her log. Del Corio followed at 10:27. Craig finally jumped off the boat at 10:37.

With a ten-minute head start, the first two divers would have to finish their dives before Craig. They would not dive as a three-man team after all.

Craig had decided to explore the *Andrea Doria* alone.

Two

STAR SHIP

During any voyage, Captain Piero Calamai had a standing order that he be summoned in the event of fog. So there he stood, on the bridge of the *Andrea Doria*, on the intermittently foggy afternoon of July 25, 1956. At times such as these, the sun hangs like a white glazed plate on a white wall, occasionally glimpsed through the peaks of mist.

Calamai was unsurprised and unperturbed. He was fifty-eight years old, a 1916 graduate of the Genoa Nautical Institute, a decorated veteran of both world wars, and the only man to command the 697-foot *Andrea Doria* since its celebrated maiden cruise three years before. This voyage marked his fortieth Atlantic crossing aboard the pride of the Italian Line.

He knew that during July in the North Atlantic, as one guided a ship west toward Nantucket Island and into New York–bound shipping lanes, fog was more likely to be present than not. Warm air moved from the East Coast of the United States and mingled there with the frigid water of the Labrador current. The result of these conditions was that the *Andrea Doria* sailed in thick sheets of fog, then clear air, then fog, and so on. The situation, though not alarming, called for professional caution. Calamai's drill was well honed. He ordered subordinates to activate the closure of twelve watertight doors belowdecks, to switch on one of the two radar units, to sound the foghorn, which would blast automatically for six seconds every hundred seconds and, finally, to reduce the liner's speed from 23 knots to 21.8.

At 6 P.M., Calamai ordered the second radar set to be turned on. It was the last night before the *Andrea Doria* was scheduled to arrive in New York, and Calamai might have been expected to make the rounds of the ship's ballrooms and lounges, where many passengers enjoyed the last evening of their nine-day voyage aboard the world's most beautiful ocean liner. He was, however, a taciturn man, not naturally talented in the small talk of the lounge tables, and at 7:30 he had a light dinner brought to him on the darkening bridge. When the icy sun finally set and the patchy fog seemed to knit together more, Calamai ordered his lookout to move forward, down from a post on the ship's mast to the bow.

In fog, a ship's crew can feel they are sailing the only ship on earth, but the waters south of Nantucket were in fact a bustling junction for transatlantic travel. At 8 P.M., the *Doria* passed within sight of the *Cape Ann*, a four-hundred-foot freighter owned by the United Fruit Company returning to New York from Bremerhaven, Germany. Tailing the *Andrea Doria* in a westbound lane a few miles south was the *Private William H. Thomas*, an American troopship also headed to New York. Coming down into the area from the northeast was the *Robert E. Hopkins*, a 425-foot oil tanker bound from Boston to Corpus Christi, Texas. About forty miles farther east steamed the 793-foot *Ile de France*, a much-beloved passenger ship that had been sailing on the Atlantic for thirty years. The *Ile de France*, bound for Plymouth, England, then Le Havre, France, had left a Hudson River pier in New York at 11:30 that morning. Another ship had left at the same time from another dock nearby, and that ship had followed the *Ile de France* out of New York Harbor.

As soon as the two ships were on the ocean, the much faster, much larger French vessel left the other far behind.

The other ship was the Swedish passenger liner *Stockholm*. At 8:30 P.M., ninety miles west of the *Andrea Doria*, the *Stockholm* sailed in clear weather and under a moon that at dusk appeared full and bright and flawless, except for one thin slice that had been pared off.

Sixty-three-year-old Captain Gunnar Nordenson, American born but reared in Sweden, had been at sea for forty-five years. Perceived as a disciplinarian to those who served under him, Nordenson had conducted a quietly successful career as a captain of passenger liners. His minutes of fame came during World War II, when he became master of the *Gripsholm*. The White Mercy Ship, as the *Gripsholm* was called, transported thousands of refugees and Allied prisoners of war from Europe to safe ports, including those in neutral Sweden. Nordenson had earned a commendation from the United States in 1945 for his actions several months earlier when, after his Samaritan vessel had been forced into occupied Norway by a German warship, he managed to get the *Gripsholm* and all passengers safely released.

The bridge crew of the *Stockholm* was now under the command of Third Officer Joan-Ernst Carstens-Johannsen. He was twenty-six, born of an upper-class family, as easygoing a man as Nordenson was sphinxian. The voyage marked his fourth Atlantic crossing. As was his habit, Carstens, as the young officer was known, checked the radar scope when his shift began. No blips, anywhere.

He adhered the *Stockholm* to the course ordered by

Nordenson, a track in the direct path of oncoming, westbound ships. Like others who commanded ships bound for northern European ports, Nordenson routinely plotted the *Stockholm* well north of the eastbound lane recommended by an international agreement. If he instead took his ship hard by the Nantucket Lightship, a stationary vessel posted to warn mariners of the dangerous Nantucket Shoals, he could point the *Stockholm* on a more direct angle to Sweden and thus save on fuel. The captain had safely made more than four hundred Atlantic crossings— half of them headed east in the westbound shipping lanes.

Nordenson made a final check on his bridge crew at 9 P.M. He estimated visibility at five miles. The darkness had deepened, and moonshine flashed like drops of mercury on the calm seas. He had Carstens tweak the course a bit farther north. Now the *Stockholm* would pass within one mile of the lightship. Before returning to his cabin, Nordenson asked Carstens to call him when the ship drew closer to the lightship. Of course, he should also be summoned in case of fog.

The *Stockholm* was a rather chilly passenger liner, a hard wooden chair to the *Doria's* overstuffed chaise. Until a few months earlier, when it had been fitted with stabilizers, the Swedish ship for years had labored with the reputation as a nausea-inducing "roller" as it picked its way across its cold-water routes. Although the stabilizers had corrected the ship's formerly rollicking motion, the *Stockholm* remained a plodder. At a maximum speed of 18.5 knots, it was significantly slower than the *Doria*.

Still, the ship possessed a severe beauty, derived from decoration and design rooted in simplicity. The *Stockholm* was all white, except for its single funnel, painted a creamy yellow. All decks were enclosed, which gave the ship the streamlined appearance of a contemporary yacht. In an advertised first for passenger liners, each of the *Stockholm*'s cabins had at least one porthole with an ocean view. The ship's architects made their most obvious concession to style with the *Stockholm*'s rakishly angled bow. Even this possessed a sober purpose: to smash through North Atlantic ice.

If, however, the *Stockholm* was a solid, faintly recognizable citizen in the society of ocean liners, the *Andrea Doria* was an unabashed celebrity, an elegant and charismatic ambassador of Italian style at midcentury.

With World War II ended, and with Marshall Plan dollars pumping into Europe, Italy's economic "miracle" took hold in the 1950s. The industrial surge was accompanied by a parallel celebration of the Italian spirit. The classic films of auteurs such as Federico Fellini and Michelangelo Antonioni played to worldwide praise (and the 1953 American film *Roman Holiday* was a visual poem celebrating Italy's capital). As Rome's *cinecitta* film-production district attracted Hollywood's movie-making crews, Milan flowered as the export capital of Italian couture.

The *Andrea Doria*, launched in 1951 and placed in service two years later, served as notice to the world that Italian ship-building, its storied yards annihilated by Allied bombers during World War II, was rebuilding. In the 1930s, swift Italian liners such as the *Rex* had established the "sunny southern route" across the Atlantic to North America. Then they were destroyed one by one in the war. In the 1950s, the government-subsidized fleets of Lloyd Triestino, Adriatica, Tirrenia, and the Italian Line would again compete on the world scale as powerful forces of commerce and maritime style. The Italian Line spent twenty-five million dollars to build and outfit the *Doria*. The timing for such a substantial investment, while not perfect, wasn't bad. In the mid-1950s, passenger-jet travel was rapidly expanding, but had not yet supplanted the ocean liner as the long-distance transportation of choice. A sustained speed of twenty-three knots along the market-tested southern route—six carefree days to New York from Naples—was the preferred pace. For at least a few more years, first-class passage on a transatlantic ship remained mass transportation's sweetest luxury, and the world offered no more sumptuous vessel on which to sail than the *Andrea Doria*.

At the Ansaldo Shipyards in Genoa, the *Doria*'s designers had painted the ship's hull black, angled its bow sharply, plated its stern curvaceously, and shaped its single funnel so that the front was higher than the rear. Taken together, these were the motifs of naval architecture that suggested speed and maneuverability. In profile, the *Doria* suggested the snappy Fiat 8V sports car of the time: Its bow section was long and low, and the white superstructure rose in well-proportioned, stair-step gradations, fore to aft.

Inside, the Andrea's *Doria* decorators had mounted a visual-arts opera, with bright arias in every media expressing the historic range of Italian art. Deep, alluding bows were made to masters of every age, from Michelangelo to the modern enamelist Paolo di Poli. Photo-accurate murals of medieval Florence and Siena decorated the cabin-class dining room. Seven-hundred-pound ceramics by Romano Rui hung on the banked walls of the Winter Garden lounge. Other surfaces in the thirty-one public rooms sparkled with huge panels of hand-hammered copper and with original tapestries. A single, mammoth mosaic was pieced together with French hickory, lemon wood, cherry, maple, and myrtle brier. The ripe collage of styles hit many passengers as soon as they walked aboard the ship, into the first-class foyer. Here, under ultramodern recessed lighting, with one wall bejeweled with an abstract ceramic straight out of a *Star Trek* episode, and before a trompe l'oeil mural of a Genovese courtyard, stood the life-sized figure of the ship's namesake, cast in bronze, in his medieval armor, right hand at the hilt of his admiral's sword. This was the No. 1 snapshot stop onboard.

"The *Andrea Doria*," cooed a promotional booklet produced by the Italian Line, was nothing less than "a ship built around a painting."

"How do you take the coldness out of steel?" read one widely produced magazine advertisement. "How do you breathe life into glass and tile? You won't find the answer in blueprints. You can't do it with money or calloused hands. You build such a ship with your heart. Every mural, every tapestry, every rug and chair . . . each exquisite bit of glassware and every glowing tile is the work of craftsmen. Yes, a ship is built of many hearts. This is the tradition of Italy. This is the *Andrea Doria*."

Because the line between brilliant decoration and mere frippery blurred on the *Andrea Doria*, it would have been easy to mistake the ship for a mere "glamour liner," as the maritime press described it. In fact, the ship's infrastructure for luxury also was indisputably up to date. Here was the first liner ever built with swimming pools for cabin, tourist, and first class. Also for each class, the ship offered separate movie theaters, ballrooms, dining rooms, lounges, card rooms, gymnasiums, and even deck promenades. The ship was entirely air-conditioned, and first-class cabins had individual temperature controls. On B Deck, the ship had a fifty-car, air-conditioned garage, where vehicles could be sealed off from the salt air. There, the Chrysler Corporation stored the hundred-thousand-dollar "Norseman," a show car built by the famed Ghia design shop in Turin, Italy, featuring an ultramodern cantilevered roof requiring no supporting pillars. The *Andrea Doria* also carried three hundred ship-to-shore telephones, an unprecedented number for the time.

Much admired by the public, the *Andrea Doria* simultaneously attracted respect from maritime insiders. In the dawning age of supersonic jets, the *Doria*'s status as one of the fastest ocean liners across the Atlantic did not make the popular impact it might had made fifty years earlier, but for the travel industry this achievement remained significant. The *Doria*'s speed meant that the Italian Line could make good on its promise of "express service" between New York and Italy. More speed meant more trips, with more passengers and more money in the bank. The ship's engines thundered with fifty thousand horsepower, and in 1951 the *Doria*'s twin propellers pushed the thirty-thousand-ton vessel to 25.3 knots in trials on the Gulf of Genoa. Besides the power belowdecks, the ship's superstructure was fabricated from sheets of aluminum, a decision that lightened the load and made more speed possible.

Its safety technology was also state of the art. Sixteen aluminum lifeboats could accommodate more than two thousand people, which exceeded the ship's capacity for passengers and crew. Like other famous ships that sank, the *Andrea Doria*, of course, was also billed as virtually "unsinkable," and in the *Doria*'s case the claim seemed well supported. The ship had been, in effect, double bottomed, with a series of fuel and water tanks from bow to stern. Hydraulically controlled doors could be closed to create eleven watertight chambers. The compartments had been sized in such a way that two of them could become flooded and the others would retain enough air to keep the ship afloat.

Only a freakish direct hit that pierced the protective line of water and fuel tanks could let in enough water to destabilize the *Andrea Doria*.

By around 10 P.M. on July 25, 1956, the *Stockholm* had knifed into the fog massed around the Nantucket Lightship, which now lay forty miles away. Like the *Andrea Doria*, the *Stockholm* now proceeded in unpredictable banks of moisture. The horizon to the north was a smudgy brushstroke through the ridges of swirling fog.

Carstens, the third officer in command on the *Stockholm*'s bridge, used the ship's radio direction finder to confirm his suspicion that the strong ocean current had pulled the ship subtly off course. The ship was tracking almost three miles north of Captain Nordenson's proscribed path. If the *Stockholm* maintained the course, it would pass too closely to the Nantucket Lightship. So at 10:30, Carstens ordered the helmsman to execute a correction of two degrees to the right. The ship's speed of 18.5 knots was maintained.

Unseen to those on the *Stockholm*'s bridge, the mammoth *Ile de France* was up ahead. Aboard were more than 1,700 passengers and crew. It was six miles to the south and passing abeam of the Nantucket Lightship as it roared east on its way to England.

A few minutes later, after replotting the *Stockholm*, Carstens ordered another correction. This steered the ship again modestly to the right, away from the lightship.

Then, within minutes of 11 P.M., Carstens checked the radar screen and saw a yellow pip.

Another ship was nearby and it was closing in.

The scope indicated that the ship was within twelve miles and perhaps two degrees to the port, or left, of the *Stockholm*. This meant that the other ship was on a virtually parallel course—or head-on—with the *Stockholm*. Minutes passed. Carstens again plotted the oncoming ship as it approached within six miles. He calculated that the ship would pass within half a mile to one mile of the *Stockholm*. He knew this passing distance would be too close for Captain Nordenson, who wanted his bridge crew to keep the *Stockholm* at least one mile from any other ship at sea. Carstens made preparations to turn the *Stockholm* to the right, away from the other vessel, to increase the passing distance. He wanted to see the ship with his own eyes before turning the *Stockholm*, however, so he walked outside on the bridge wings. He saw no ship. When the radar appeared to indicate that the oncoming ship had pulled to within four miles, Carstens switched the *Stockholm*'s radar set from fifteen-mile range to five-mile range.

He returned to the bridge wing. Still, he saw no ship.

The *Andrea Doria* had passed the Nantucket Lightship at 10:20. Unlike Nordenson, Captain Calamai remained on the bridge as his ship traveled in fog. He had changed into his evening blue uniform and matching beret. Earlier in the day, the *Doria* had been six hours behind schedule for its arrival into New York. Now, Calamai estimated, he was only one hour behind schedule. Though sailing now for seven hours in an ever-thickening batting of fog, Calamai maintained the ship's speed at 21.8 knots.

It was debatable whether Calamai's almost token reduction in speed earlier in the day rose to the spirit of the International Regulations for Preventing Collision at Sea. They said ships should maintain a "reasonable" pace, defined as a speed at which the ship could come to a complete stop in half the distance of visibility. Visibility was so poor that Calamai ordered Second Officer Curzio Franchini to check the radar more frequently. But if he strictly obeyed the regulations, to which the Italian Line did not officially ascribe anyway (neither did the Swedish Line), Calamai would literally make no headway at all. That he would simply stop the *Andrea Doria* in the middle of the ocean was not an option. The "regulations," the product of years of deliberations by professional mariners and shipping officials, were, in the practical world, mere recommendations. Calamai was behind schedule, and he had bills to pay.

Then, at 10:45, a pip materialized on the *Andrea Doria*'s radar screen. Calamai's bridge officers estimated the pip to apparently represent a boat seventeen miles away and a few degrees to the right. It wasn't clear at first that the pip necessarily represented a ship, much less an ocean liner.

Now, as the minutes ticked away, the pip's movement across the screen indicated a fast ship approaching the *Doria* from the opposite direction. Calamai's crew, watching the pip, told Calamai the ship was moving at an angle that was increasing to the right of the *Andrea Doria*. Second Officer Franchini said the two ships might pass within one mile of each other. As the other ship closed the gap, Franchini switched the ship's radar scope from twenty-mile range down to an eight-mile radius.

Maritime custom called for ships to pass each other port-to-port—with the port side of one ship running past the port side of the other vessel. However, starboard passings were deemed reasonable if the two ships were on parallel courses with insufficient room, or time, to maneuver for a port-to-port. Calamai prepared for a starboard-to-starboard passing.

Franchini estimated the oncoming ship at four to five miles away. The pip fattened a bit on screen. The other ship was apparently a large one, just like the *Doria*. Calamai moved back and forth between the wheelhouse and the bridge wing. If the two ships were to pass within one mile, he wanted to confirm what was happening on the radar scope with his own eyes. He wanted to see the other ship.

He stood on the bridge wing and peered into the mist. Still, he saw no ship.

The men on the bridge could hear the muffled musical bass line pulsing from one deck below, where dancers in the Belvedere Lounge were enjoying the cheerful stylings of Dino Massa and his orchestra. Most of the public rooms on the ship were quiet, but the small Belvedere was packed. The full name of the room was the Belvedere Observation Lounge, so named for the banks of windows on three sides that afforded a panoramic view of the sea. Now the windowpanes were blackened, the stars erased by the fog. Among the crowd that night had been some of the better-known passengers who lent the *Andrea Doria* some of its cachet.

Richardson Dilworth and his wife, Ann, had been relaxing in the lounge. He was the newly elected mayor of Philadelphia, a decorated marine who had survived the savage combat of Guadalcanal. Silver haired, Dilworth's commanding presence appeared to have lifted him above hurdles that in that era often proved politically fatal—a divorce and his acknowledged struggle with alcoholism. One of the cabins across the hall from Dilworth and his wife was occupied by actress Ruth Roman. She was dancing in the lounge at about 11, and she was, as the movie press said, raven haired. Thirty-two years old, with twenty films to her credit, Roman was a Warner Brothers leading lady who generally got the good-girl roles; five years earlier she had appeared in *Strangers on a Train*, one of Aldred Hitchcock's edgier films. She was traveling with her three-year-old son, Dickie, and his babysitter. Also aboard were Hungarian dancers Nora Kovach and her husband, Istvan Rabovsky, who had made headlines three years earlier when they defected to the West; their book, *Leap Through the Curtain,* had been published five months earlier.

In the cabin-class dining room, about two hundred passengers were seated watching *Foxfire,* a Jeff Chandler/Jane Russell vehicle in which Chandler once again portrayed a man of combined European and American Indian descent. On another deck, children watched a Walt Disney film. A second band played to dancers on the Promenade Deck. Generally, however, a winding-down atmosphere had settled on the ship as it splashed through the dark waves. In the card room next to the Belvedere Lounge, three priests played Scrabble. The purser's office quietly bustled as people retrieved money and valuables they had stored there for safekeeping. A few passengers squared away their luggage on the Promenade Deck. They had been instructed to stack it there in preparation for the next morning's arrival into New York.

Just past 11, the fog finally yielded to Carstens a view of the unknown ship headed his way. At first, the sight was ghostly. The ship's form was not yet visible, but its signal lights threw off faint glows, as if the ghost were beckoning with lanterns.

"Lights to port," Carstens finally said to his crew.

He did not order the *Stockholm* slowed or the foghorn activated. Through binoculars, Carstens saw two white mast lights and a red light—the red light being the portside light of the approaching ship. Starboard lights shine green. The ship, then, was traveling to the left of the *Stockholm*. *Stockholm's* radar showed the other ship moving in from about 1.8 miles away. Carstens estimated that the ship's course would take it past the *Stockholm* at a distance of six-tenths of a mile. Too close. He ordered the helmsman to turn the Swedish ship to the right, to increase the passing distance.

As the *Stockholm's* bow almost imperceptibly tracked to the right, Carstens returned to the bridge wing and lifted the binoculars to his eyes. He was stunned. Now, instead of seeing the red port light, he saw the green starboard light.

The other ship was turning across the bow of the *Stockholm*.

Hundreds of portholes suddenly blinked open across the narrowing channel between the two ships.

At 11:05, Captain Calamai had ordered the helmsman to turn the *Andrea Doria* slightly to the left because the radar scope indicated that the approaching ship was off to the right. Slowly, the distance between the ships increased to about two miles. Calamai saw the green light of the ship's starboard side. So it appeared to be veering away from the *Doria's* path.

While the *Andrea Doria* continued to blast its automatic foghorn, the *Stockholm* continued to travel in silence. A few minutes later, Calamai used binoculars and saw that the other ship had closed to within one mile. He looked for the green light again, but couldn't see it.

Then he saw the oncoming ship's portside red light.

The other ship was turning straight toward the *Andrea Doria*.

"Hard-a-port!" Calamai shouted.

Seaman Giulio Visiano spun the helm like a roulette wheel. The ship responded slowly and began to track left. Calamai maintained his speed to help the ship maneuver. With 21.8 knots speed, the *Doria* rolled to the left and the right side of the ship rose up. It was 11:09.

The *Stockholm*'s ice-breaking prow exploded into the side of the *Andrea Doria*. The forward tip of the *Stockholm* drilled thirty feet into the *Doria*, ripping through bulkheads, smashing bunks, and slicing through thin tubes that immediately hemmorhaged oil and hydraulic fluids.

Aboard the *Andrea Doria*, the Walt Disney film being shown in one theater jumped a few frames before stopping. In the Belvedere Lounge, Dino Massa's boys were playing "Arrivederci Roma" and some of the musicians lost their place, then ceased playing as glasses crashed to the floor, and tables and chairs began rocketing across the room, as if magnetized to the starboard wall. The ship shuddered from stem to stern. The steel emitted a long groan.

The plates of the two ships melted together for about ten seconds in a screeching embrace, until they were pried apart by the forces opposite the momentum that joined them.

Disgorged, with seventy-five feet of its clipper bow looking as though a bomb had detonated there, the *Stockholm* then scraped some three hundred feet along the length of the *Doria's* black hull, igniting a trail of sparks that sizzled like a fuse in the foggy night. Then the ships veered away from each other, absent all control, lights out.

Starting at a point just below the *Andrea Doria's* bridge wings, painted a brilliant white, the ship's open wound was an isosceles triangle, about forty feet at the top and progressively narrowing to the lowest deck with passenger accommodations, C Deck, then two more decks to the ship's bottom. Of the *Andrea Doria's* eleven decks, seven had been ripped open. Seawater poured into the lower decks.

"*Santo vergine,*" said Francesco De Girolamo, a C Deck passenger who was moving his family to New York from Ischia, Italy. "*Siamo andati sugli scogli?*" Holy Virgin. Have we hit the rocks?

De Girolamo whirled toward one of his three sons, Antonio, seventeen. Italy's tectonic plates shifted routinely, and to them the collision felt like an earthquake.

"Dad, *what* rocks?" Antonio responded. "We're in the middle of the ocean."

Antonio rushed to a porthole at the end of the short hall outside the cabin. The ocean, normally dark as the ship traveled in the night, was ablaze.

"Dad, there are lights out there," Antonio said when he returned. "It looks like another ship. We have hit another ship!"

Soon Francesco De Girolamo and his wife, Anna, and the couple's five children were making their way through long, dark passageways packed with other scared passengers. Their feet grew cold from the water steadily rising in the halls. The air smelled of oil and the ocean.

When the De Girolamos reached the Promenande Deck, the bottoms of their pant legs and dress hems blackened with oil that had begun to mix with water in the passageways, a surprisingly subdued but palpably tense scene was unfolding. There were piles of next-day luggage everywhere on the Promenade. The ship now tilted more than twenty degrees. The fog was so thick that people could not see from the portside railing to the starboard rail, a distance of ninety feet. A strange quiet prevailed. The ship's engines were stopped, and the fog dampened all sound, including the screams of the panicked. Captain Calamai's officers had issued few announcements, other than a reminder to passengers that they grab their life belts. Then an electrical generator roared to life, and it was so deafening that instructions would be delivered in increasingly hoarse shouts from the crew members.

The fog droplets slickened the deck. Several people lost their grip on the high-side rail—on the portside—and slid helplessly across the sloping deck until they smashed into the low side. These mishaps multiplied because large numbers of people had naturally gravitated to the high side of the deck but then had to negotiate their way to the low side, because that was the only place lifeboats could be lowered, or where people could board lifeboats soon to arrive from other ships.

The sights through the early hours of the morning were at once spectacular, terrifying, and slow moving. The first ship to respond to the *Andrea Doria*'s distress transmission was the *Cape*

Ann, the freighter traveling from Germany to New York. The *Cape Ann*, which was fifteen miles southeast of the collision when it occurred, had only two lifeboats. It got to the scene at 12:30. The U.S. military transport, *Private William H. Thomas*, was nineteen miles east of the crash; the *Thomas* turned around and sped to the scene, with the captain intending to deploy only the ship's two motorized lifeboats in the interest of speed. The *Thomas* drew near to the listing *Doria* at about 1:30.

On the deck of the *Doria*, more than seventeen hundred people snaked in single-file lines to places where the small boats approached. Most passengers waited their turns calmly, even as the *Doria*'s funnel slowly tipped over their heads until it was nearly parallel with the surface of the ocean. They could see the bottoms of the swimming pools, now turned toward them. People sat because the list was so severe.

Then, just before 2 A.M., the mountainous *Ile de France* slowed to a stop some four hundred yards from the stricken *Andrea Doria*. Headed to France, the ship had been forty-four miles east of the collision site when Captain Raoul de Beaudean decided to turn around. De Beaudean's ship was the grande dame of the French passenger fleet, launched in 1926 and famed for her luxurious art deco interiors and exquisite cuisine. In World War II, the *Ile de France* had comfortably ferried thousands of Allied troops, and a 1949 refitting had knocked back the ship's old-style rank of three funnels to a more contemporary two. If the *Andrea Doria* was the ingénue in the constellation of passenger liners, then the *Ile de France* was the aging star, a featured player still quite beautiful and in full possession of her talents. Now, aboard the glamorous giant, all engines were stopped. Then, with a flick of a few switches, its entire exterior suddenly lit up. Ten-foot-high block letters spelling ILE DE FRANCE, suspended between the ship's stacks, shined brightly through the fog. Spirits lifted among the survivors, and among the crews on the smaller ships struggling to rescue those who still needed help.

"Through the mist across a gentle rolling stretch of water was a great ocean liner [the *Ile de France*], its every cabin alight and looking for all the world like an island city rising out of the fog," wrote survivor David Hollyer, on the occasion of the sinking's twenty-fifth anniversary, in 1981. "Playing down upon the intervening space between the two vessels, powerful searchlights illuminated the scene."

The *Ile de France* would take on 753 passengers and crew from the disaster. In all, seventeen hundred passengers and crew were rescued from the *Andrea Doria* by the *Ile de France* and the other ships that abandoned their intineraries and rushed to the emergency.

The *Andrea Doria's* engine rooms were flooded by midnight. The *Stockholm* had heavily damaged three compartments, those containing the *Andrea Doria's* cargo hold, generator room, and deep fuel tanks. The ship had been designed to survive the breaching of two compartments, but not three. The right side of the ship sagged inexorably to the sea's surface.

Calamai remained aboard through the seven hours it took to take everyone else off the ship. He pinned his hope on the arrival of U.S. Coast Guard tugboats, which he hoped could tow the ship to a place where it could be grounded and perhaps repaired. But, as other officers told him, the tugs were hours away. It was no longer safe to be aboard the *Andrea Doria*.

Calamai finally allowed himself to be escorted off his ship at 5:30 A.M.

He went aboard the U.S. Coast Guard buoy-tender *Hornbeam*. He was almost mute. Twelve hours earlier he had been the skipper of his proud nation's proudest ship. His stature approached the mythical. When he spoke on the *Hornbeam*, it was to repeatedly ask others why the *Stockholm* had turned as it did, when it did. Why no warning whistle? Why no foghorn?

It was just after 10 A.M. when the ship finally slid under the waves. The words ANDREA DORIA and GENOA remained visible on the stern for a few minutes before they were obscured by the whirlpool that churned around the sinking ship. A tide of debris bobbed on the currents: hundreds of deck chairs, suitcases, shards of the smashed lifeboats. As the ship descended, an immense field of bioluminescence emerged in the ship's shape at the surface, as if the *Doria*'s spirit was escaping before the ship slammed into the sand and mud below. At least twenty feet of the ship piled below the seafloor before she came to rest on her starboard side at a depth of 250 feet.

After watching the wrenching scene, Calamai asked the Coast Guard whether he could send a telegram from the *Hornbeam* to the Italian Line headquarters in New York. They said he could, of course.

He was brief.

"*Doria* sank 10:09—Calamai."

Almost all of the fifty-one people who died in the catastrophe died at the moment of impact.

On the *Stockholm*, five crew members died, including three

seamen asleep in their spartan cabins in their ship's narrow bow section. Their bodies were swept overboard when the *Stockholm*'s seven-hundred-foot anchor chains, freed when the locker containing them burst open on impact, unwound and dragged the men into the ocean.

Picking his way through the twisted wreckage of the *Stockholm*'s bow, a crewman heard a child's voice calling for her mother. The faint cries belonged to Linda Morgan, a fourteen-year-old *Andrea Doria* passenger who had been catapulted by the collision through the fog and onto the *Stockholm*. She survived.

Forty-six *Andrea Doria* passengers died, forty-two of them on impact or soon thereafter. People either were crushed as the *Stockholm* crashed through bulkheads and staterooms or were trapped and drowned when the *Andrea Doria* quickly listed some twenty degrees, sending the cold water of the Atlantic pouring into the lower decks.

Although the *Doria* dead were sprinkled on most of the ship's decks, the largest group of victims perished on C Deck, where berths fetched the cheapest price. Twenty-six people died in the cabin-class staterooms of C Deck. Here were located most of the Italian families with young children, the majority of them on their way to America to begin new lives.

Evaporating the events on July 25, 1956, to their essence, and considering all the arguments forwarded by maritime experts, the collision apparently occurred because the westbound *Andrea Doria* was going too fast and because the bridge crew aboard the eastbound *Stockholm* misread its radar set.

Of the two key factors, the former was by far the lesser transgression. If ships in that era kept to prescribed speed "limits" in fog, few would ever have made their schedules, and an Atlantic sailing with no fog was a rarity. But the fog that night seemed to have been uncommonly intense. Captain Raoul de Beaudean of the *Ile de France* reported that as he stood on the bridge of his ship, he could not see its bow. It's a puzzle why Calamai did not slow down even more when he knew another ship approached.

The community of navigation experts who remain captivated by the bizarre accident have found it difficult to understand why neither of the captains involved—or in the *Stockholm*'s case, Carstens—made bolder turns at earlier points in the ships' slowly unfolding encounter. The *Doria*'s radar picked up the *Stockholm* from seventeen miles away, and the *Stockholm* saw the *Doria*'s blip twelve miles away. Both ships had roughly thirty minutes' time to respond and get out of each other's way. From the beginning, it was apparent the two liners were headed on a parallel course, more or less bow-to-bow toward each other. Each crew verified the parallel course with radar, dead reckoning, and, in the case of the *Andrea Doria*, by plotting the ships on charts in the old-fashioned way. Yet, as if a high-stakes game of chicken were the aim, both bridges seemed determined to guide the ships past each other at generous speed with only minimal passing distance.

The *Andrea Doria*'s crew absorbed the brunt of criticism in the early years. Many attributed this to anti-Italian bias and to the presence in the first lifeboats leaving the stricken ship of a disturbing number of *Doria* crew members. Captain Calamai's reputation was permanently tarnished by his failure to slow his ship more dramatically, given the low-visibility conditions and by his failure to accomplish a standard, port-to-port passing.

In recent years, however, the performance of the *Stockholm*'s crew has drawn increasing scrutiny. Many experts always believed the disaster would have been averted had the relatively inexperienced Carstens simply summoned his veteran skipper as he realized another ship would be approaching close by. One newer school of thought also argues that Carstens, left on his own, made a series of critical errors in radar interpretation. John Carrothers, a navigation expert and also a former watch engineer with the United States Lines, originally put this argument forward. Captain Robert Meurn, a former sea captain who now teaches bridge watchstanding at the U.S. Merchant Marine Academy expanded and refined the theory.

Radar scopes of that era bore a series five concentric rings, and they also had range scales, twelve-mile and five-mile. They were equipped with big knobs off to the side of the screen to change the scale. Operators used flashlights to see what range they were on (the bridges, as are bridges today, were kept dark so the crew could see out).

In testimony at the official inquiry in New York, Carstens claimed that he first saw the *Andrea Doria*'s pip at 11:05 P.M.—four minutes before the eventual collision—on the fourth ring of the radar scope. On the fifteen-mile scale, a ship that appeared on the fourth ring was twelve miles out.

But on the five-mile scale, a fourth-ring ship was only four miles away. To Meurn, it's clear that Carstens misread the radar.

When Carstens turned the ship right to increase the passing distance with a ship he believed was twelve miles distant, Meurn argues, he in fact turned the *Stockholm* into the path of a ship only four miles away.

With both ships moving at high speed, Carstens's apparent error was not correctable.

At first, the divers found themselves surrounded by jellyfish. Hundreds of jellyfish.

Saucer-topped and trailing their glassy tentacles, the jellyfish seemed to float from everywhere with the current, as if they were being routed by something far below. At fifty feet below the sea's surface, the water turned cooler. The jellyfish disappeared. They remained above the divers, where it was warm. At irregular intervals, globules of black oil rose around the divers. The blobs looked like flights of balloons, visibly fattening from the steadily reducing pressure as they ascended to the surface where, the men had seen minutes before, they burst into in oval-shaped patches. The oil was draining drop by drop from the wreck of the *Andrea Doria*.

It was seventeen days after the sinking. *Life* magazine had arrived. An editor for the magazine, Kenneth MacLeish, along with department store heir and adventurer Peter Gimbel, mounted the expedition. They had with them three young, hotshot divers from the U.S. Navy Electronics Laboratory in San Diego. It was the age of the test pilot, and these Navy men packed "aqualungs," the experimental forerunner to modern scuba gear. The West Coast divers included Robert F. Dill, who would one day become a famous scientist at the Scripps Institute of Oceanography. The MacLeish project was a follow-up to a breakneck enterprise undertaken by Gimbel on July 28 in which he and another man, Joseph Fox, sped to the collision site to get photographs of the new shipwreck. They succeeded, but only after a harrowing episode during which Fox, at 160 feet, appeared to weaken or faint. He and Gimbel then shot straight to the surface from that depth and somehow avoided a hit of decompression sickness. A July 29 headline in the *New York Times:*

2 SKIN-DIVERS VIEW

THE *DORIA* AND FIND

HER 'ALMOST ALIVE'

Of the *Andrea Doria*, Gimbel told the newspaper, "She is lying on her starboard side and her port side seems in excellent condition. Her paint isn't even blemished. The portholes are unbroken. Even the lights along the promenade deck are unbroken."

Gimbel's photographs—he took only eight—were spread over successive issues of *Life*. But the magazine wanted more. MacLeish was a swashbuckling character, having, among other underwater adventures, once descended to seven thousand feet in a French bathysphere.

The divers found that the *Andrea Doria*, which sailed on the ocean's surface with such grace and distinction, had settled on the bottom with relatively little fuss. Unlike so many other famous wrecks, such as the *Britannic*, the ship had not broken up on impact with the sandy ocean floor. It had not settled on its keel, which is the preferred orientation for any wreck to be explored by scuba divers. But it rested cleanly on its stricken starboard side, with rows of portside windows offering themselves up for the inevitable recreational scavenging.

Inside the ship, curtains rolled in the watery breeze. The divers found that every surface was coated with a marine slime so thin that the brightwork around portholes still gleamed, and the teak decks still glowed. Furniture was suspended in the ship's ballrooms and lounges. Baggage had piled up on the Promenade Deck, exactly where it had been left seventeen days earlier. Shoes, taken off by many passengers to secure their footing on the foggy night of the sinking, littered the deck. A ring of keys still hung in a lock. The quiet was interrupted randomly by the crash of glass from cabinets and pans from kitchen shelves. A few lifeboats somehow survived the fast descent, and the divers found sharks nestled inside.

A couple of the divers were near an elevator shaft when they were unnerved by a series of booms. The ship shuddered, just as it did when the *Stockhom* hit. The *Doria's* steel plates, somewhere, were collapsing. They divers swam out of the ship and to the bridge. One of them, obviously feeling the intoxicating effect of being two hundred feet underwater for fifteen minutes, tried in vain to unbolt a searchlight with his fingers.

The unbroken process of artifact removal, which would stretch forty years long, had begun.

Dill swam about in awe. He thought the ship looked trim and ready for service. It all looked so fresh and so pure, Dill thought; why was it here? He felt sickened. The sense of awe was mixed, however, with a determination to grab things. Dill made his way into the bridge and removed a mahogany riser on which the ship's helmsman had stood.

Gimbel picked up a suitcase before he ascended. On the boat later, he popped the case and found rosaries and souvenir trinkets from Italy, and identification; the bag belonged to Justine Messina, of Valley Stream, New York. A few days later Gimbel, accompanied by a *Life* photographer, drove out to Long Island and presented the suitcase to Mrs. Messina. Everyone agreed it was a nice touch.

It also may have been the only time that something taken off the wreck of the *Andrea Doria* was returned to its rightful owner.

Three

C H I N A   F E V E R

In the spring of 1998, two months before his mid-June trip to the *Andrea Doria,* Craig Sicola had plucked a couple of items from the sunken wreck of the *British Freedom,* just outside Halifax Harbor. It was an oil tanker that had been torpedoed and sunk in 220 feet of water by the Germans during World War II. Checking the digital readout on his wrist, which told him how long he had been on the wreck, he saw he was nearing the end of the dive. He swam along the outside of the old ship, looking for the line that was tied into the wreck, and which led to the charter boat on the surface. He couldn't find it.

Craig was in Halifax with other customers of Atlantic Divers, the shop near Atlantic City operated by Gene Peterson, a diver well known in the Northeast wreck-diving community. Peterson liked to take customers up to the Halifax Harbor wrecks to prepare for *Doria* charters. He also liked Craig. The dive shop owners were friends with many of their customers. The shop owners sold masks and air tank fills and expensive dry suits, but they also marketed enduring skills and a lifestyle. They spent many weekend hours together with their customers in cramped cars traveling to marinas, where they would board charter boats for more hours of uncomfortable and sometimes even dangerous travel to the diving sites.

But Craig was especially good company. He was fiery and opinionated and checked in early with his diving buddies on Long Beach Island, New Jersey, in the spring, reminding them of their "annual" trip to the *Andrea Doria*, even if they had done it only once before. A single guy, he had five telephones in his house so he wouldn't miss a call from one of his many friends, or from one of his growing number of contacts in the contracting business. His friends like a photograph from 1997 that shows him on the deck of the *Seeker* on an earlier trip: His eyes are hidden behind black Ray-Bans, and his strong shoulders pour out of a black tank top; he leans back in a plastic patio chair and his mouth gapes with the big shiny smile. "That's Craig. He was just a casual, laid-back dude," says his friend Ken Mason.

Craig was a surfer on Long Beach Island, and he embodied the blend of seemingly contradictory traits common to so many surfers. The sport required equal measures of patience and aggressiveness—patience to wile away those milky-skied mornings when the surf was small and occasional. The aggressiveness came into play when he cut back on a breaker, nosing the board momentarily toward the wave's backside, when it's simpler to simply glide along, perpendicular to the curl.

Gene Peterson liked the way Craig had grown into a student of deep diving, even if he sometimes felt the need to counsel Craig to stay within his capabilities underwater. Still, Peterson appreciated that the man had sought out sport-diving legend Billy Deans in the Florida Keys for some of his earlier training and had begun to take pride in mastering the intricacies of gas mixing. The depth, water temperature, and visibility at the ruins of the *British Freedom* were comparable to the *Andrea Doria* wreck site, and Peterson also wanted to check out some his divers on their use of the Trimix breathing gases.

It wasn't the Trimix, however, that posed a problem for Craig that cool spring day. It was his "up line," a reel of rope that deep divers keep with them in case they cannot ascend the anchor line and need to go up on their own.

On paper at least, the procedure is simple. The diver ties off one end of the line to the underwater wreck and knots the other end to a rubberized bag inflated with air from a tank on his or her back. Then the diver ascends the up line—a sort of improvised anchor line—pausing several minutes at a series of decompression stops. No one wanted to do this kind of ascent; the real anchor line was much sturdier in the current and when you eventually hit the surface with an up line, you would end up a couple of hundred feet from the boat, with a tough swim left to do before you hit the ladder. Once safely aboard, there would also be the usual brutal joshing from the other divers about having screwed up.

Many experienced Northeast divers go into the water with a "Jersey reel" attached to their rigs, often between the twin tanks on their backs; this is usually an eight-inch-wide reel wound with heavyweight sisal rope. Craig's up line was lightweight nylon. It was also cheap. It was an inexplicable exception to the rule under which Craig seemed to buy only the best diving gear, such as the pair of black Harvey's Titanium gloves he wore for the colder dives. Peterson didn't like the line. It can easily be borne away by the current, and it has a tendency to chafe when wrapped around the rusty tie-in points on the old shipwrecks. If the line chafes through and parts at the tie-in point, it means divers have to maintain their depth at the decompression stop on their own, which is extremely difficult—even if they don't have to contend with a fast-running ocean current. Divers who get into that kind of trouble are often found miles downcurrent, where they pop to the surface, their lifeless eyes red with blood vessels damaged from uncontrolled ascent. For Northeast shipwreck divers, the Jersey reel is like the mountaineer's ice axe: an essential piece of safety equipment.

"I told him many times that I didn't think it was a worthwhile system," Gene Peterson said. "It was just the line itself."

That day on the *British Freedom*, Gene Peterson's skepticism of Craig's up-line system was confirmed. Craig managed to tie off the line on the ship, but the nylon drifted and curled with the current and he became tangled up in it, like a dog in a leash. Getting caught in a tied-off rope can pose real danger for the diver, because the current can pull so hard that it can make the line snap off an air tank valve, or even turn the valve's knob, shut the tank down, and cut off the diver's air. Another of Peterson's divers had to cut Craig out of the nylon rope.

While Peterson objected to Craig's use of the cheap rope, he was even more disturbed by Craig's apparently casual attitude about how much time he had left on the wreck. Peterson knew that divers usually get into trouble when they make a series of small errors that compound each other. Craig had failed to watch the clock and had to get out fast. In a hurry, he missed the anchor line and was forced to send up his own ascent line. "I talked to Craig about doing these thing at the last minute of your dive when much more caution is advised," Peterson said.

Craig was a talented diver, but what had happened at the *British Freedom* was plain sloppiness.

After the Nova Scotia trip, Craig returned to Long Beach Island and his role as principal in Craig Sicola Builders, makers of custom homes. He would be able to squeeze in several more weeks of work before the summer crowds made it difficult get on and off the island. That's when he planned to go to the *Andrea Doria*. The homes he built cost half a million to one million dollars. Craig had excelled in mathematics at the big, regional high school in Manahawkin, and at Ocean County Community College; he enjoyed discussing the angles described by a house's internal framing, and the challenges posed by the construction of a curved exterior facade. He liked to describe to his father and stepmother the different saws he used for different wood. On the job site, Craig was a demanding boss. Not everyone on a construction site plans to bang nails their whole life, so you had to keep an eye on people, and Craig did. He was a perfectionist. If a piece of wood was a quarter inch off what the plans dictated, Craig ripped it out.

"Things were built exactly to what the plan was, more than any builder I worked with," said Mason, one of Craig's closest friends and an occasional coworker.

Craig played hard, too. He loved to ski in Colorado, and he invariably took the hardest trails. He was not a physically imposing man—five foot ten, 165 pounds—but he was strong and athletic. He had an impulsive streak that, at least to the people closest to him, was boyish and endearing. Once, at the supermarket in Ship Bottom, New Jersey, he was standing in the checkout line behind an attractive woman he had never seen before, and he asked her out. It was Karen Moscufo. They stayed together for almost eight years. Karen had a young son by a man who had died in a car accident, and Craig became a surrogate father to the boy, named Chris. Like Craig, and with Craig's tutelage, Chris developed into an excellent soccer player at the high school. Even though Craig and Karen had split up when Craig went to the *Doria* that summer of 1998, she still had a key to his place, and they saw each other on occasion. It was harder to move apart than they had anticipated.

On the morning of June 22, Craig pulled his black Ford pickup into LBI Scuba. The shop was close to the northern end of the island, and you could see the 170-foot Barnegat Lighthouse from there, not far from where he and Karen had done some diving. Craig was about to drive to Montauk, where the *Seeker* was kept during the summer weeks when Dan Crowell led the *Andrea Doria* trips. LBI was his home-base scuba shop, although he also patronized Atlantic Divers in Point Pleasant, near Atlantic City, to be a part of Gene Peterson's frequent charters. LBI Scuba owner Carol Branco looked up with a smile when Craig burst through the entrance. He loudly announced his agenda.

"I'm going to look for china!" he said.

Two of the most important women in Craig Sicola's life—his stepmother, Susan Sicola, and Karen—had mentioned to him a few times that they would love a plate from the shipwreck. Susan collected antique and unusual china, and she enjoyed serving meals from them in her gracious home in Livingston, New Jersey. Neither woman was putting in orders exactly. They just meant to be encouraging to Craig.

In part because she knew that Craig's mother had died years earlier, shop owner Carol Branco thought of Craig as a little brother. She a took a pair of Harvey's gloves off a sales rack for him. Thin layers of titanium wrapped in neoprene. She knew his hands got cold underwater, and the temperature at the *Andrea Doria* remained in the forties even in the summer months.

Cold water is only one of the hazards of Northeast wreck diving. Poor visibility is the other obvious drawback. Many divers from New Jersey and New York frequent a string of sunken ships that lie between the two states, sites known collectively as the "mudhole wrecks." On most days, you can't see much past your fins. Divers have to string lights in and out of the wrecks to see where they're going. Overcoming the obstacles makes Northeast divers tough, confident, and proud. Anyone can strap on a single and look at the pretty fish in Belize, they like to say. Try diving with a hood, thick gloves, and keeping track of five steel tanks while penetrating in an "overhead environment"—that is, inside a sunken ship or even a submarine. Divers are an odd breed. They draw their satisfaction from the nautical artifacts they raid from all the ships that wrecked on the rocky approaches to the nation's busiest chain of ports and from the knowledge that no divers in the United States deal with the challenges they face routinely. Their loose-knit fraternity draws members only when divers grow bored with less challenging charters and seek out fellow travelers, slightly crazed and comfortable hard up against what others consider the limits. For many of them, a dive of 180 feet is by definition better than a dive of 140 feet because 180 feet is deeper. Craig was one of them.

Carol Branco, who had trained divers for years, nevertheless urged Craig to execute a conservative diving plan. She reminded him that he had only been to the *Andrea Doria* once before, the previous summer.

"Yeah, yeah," he told her, "I got my plan squared away. Got it squared away."

"Who are you diving with?" Branco asked.

"Well, I'm not going to dive with anyone."

"You're diving alone?" She said it flat to make her disapproval clear.

"Yeah," he said. "All those guys out there dive alone."

Craig turned to go.

"Hey, I love you, asshole, so be careful!" Branco told Craig as he moved to the door. "Don't forget, Craig, no piece of china is worth your life."

But Craig was on his way out the door, and she wasn't sure if he had heard what she said. She heard the truck engine start. An uneasy feeling whirred inside her, and she wanted to tell him not to go.

Craig picked up his cell phone as he drove north. To get to Montauk, he would drive to New York, past the skyline of Manhattan, then east more than a hundred miles, across Queens, then the length of Long Island. It would be at least four hours, with good traffic. He called Karen Moscufo, whom he'd seen three days earlier at Chris's graduation. He got her machine.

"Hi guys, I'm on my way! I have a long drive in front of me. See you guys! Love you!"

Now he called his father, Louis Sicola, who worked in insurance. Lou was not comfortable with Craig's wreck diving. Craig's passion for water sports had not been passed down from his father, who could barely swim. Why couldn't Craig dive on reefs instead? Louis asked his son. "Borrring!" was the response. Lou had to come to understand this side of Craig. He had been with Craig when his son had met Billy Deans in Key West a few years earlier. He was so excited when he signed up for instruction with Deans, it was if Michael Jordan had agreed to provide him basketball pointers. As he drove on, Craig told his father about the series of diving trips he had lined up for the summer, and all about the new house he was building, which was nearly finished.

"I'm working hard, Dad, but I'm also having fun," Craig said.

The two men had seen each other a few days earlier, over Father's Day weekend. They talked about getting together more.

It was dark by the time Craig got to Montauk. The *Seeker* was tied up at the Star Island Marina, one of several major sportfishing marinas shouldered together on the shore of the harbor known as Lake Montauk. The Coast Guard has its station on the end of Star Island, which causeways long ago had made a peninsula. Rescue boats can quickly thread Montauk Inlet and get out to sea. The Star Island Marina uses the inlet every summer for its shark-fishing tournament; hundreds of competing boats sweep through the narrow channel at dawn in the timed event, which requires them to get back by late afternoon. The blues and threshers come back lashed to the sides of the fishing boats, leaking blood where the gaff split their sides, their tails creasing the water like skegs. Whoever gets the biggest shark wins thousands of dollars, not only in announced prizes but in lucrative private wagers.

The *Seeker* would be a familiar presence at Star Island that summer, because Dan had scheduled eleven *Andrea Doria* charters. No one had ever scheduled even half as many before. No one could doubt that the *Seeker* was the No. 1 ride to the sunken liner. Dan wasn't in port much, however. Just long enough to wash the boat down, refuel, and scrub at the oil stains at the *Seeker*'s waterline. Dan flicked on the *Seeker*'s exterior lights as his crew members and customers, including Craig Sicola, began to pull into the gravel parking lot.

In the shadows they had the hulking profiles of Sherpas, carrying fat duffel bags and air tanks that clinked together as they were carried. To avoid the cost of refilling on Dan's boat, some divers brought spare pairs of tanks, already filled with their desired blend of oxygen, nitrogen, and helium. People would go out to dinner together, then return to the *Seeker* for the ride out to sea. Invariably the Liar's Saloon across the water would be lit up, and packed, casting orange flames of light on the black water. The *Seeker* crew often visited the place when they returned from an *Andrea Doria* trip, but it wasn't safe to drink heavily before diving.

Gene Peterson, who had chartered the *Seeker* on behalf of his diving shop customers, including Craig, had already arrived when Craig appeared. Peterson didn't like what he saw. Craig was packing the same cheap up line, the reel of lightweight yellow nylon that had gotten him into trouble on the *British Freedom*.

He mentioned it to Craig. That was part of Peterson's job, really. Craig was friendly, but stubborn. The reel was fine, he insisted.

"This is one sport when you can offer advice and guidance," Peterson said, "but the person has to learn themselves."

Eighteen people, including Dan Crowell and his crew of five, were aboard the *Seeker* that night by the time Dan steered the boat through the inlet and out to the dark ocean. It would take about eight hours to get to the waters above the *Andrea Doria*. Craig was aboard with a Long Beach Island contingent that included Ken Mason, Paul Whittaker, and Jim Schultz.

"We were all attracted to it for the artifacts, first of all," said Schultz. "Then, just the challenge of it. You could say, 'I'm a *Doria* diver.' You had the bragging rights. Craig liked that. You dive the *Doria*, it means a guy knows what he's doing.'"

The *Seeker* left by 10 that night and made it to the wreck by 6:30 A.M. Dan had long ago punched in the *Andrea Doria's* coordinates on the navigation computer in the *Seeker's* wheelhouse. People tried to sleep on the voyage, which was not easy with the boat's twin, 325-horsepower Detroit Diesels churning through the night. A little before 8, two members of Dan's crew, Tom Packer and Steve Gatto, made the first dives and secured the *Seeker's* anchor line to the mooring attached to the *Andrea Doria* below. The mooring was in the same slot along the ship's bow through which the *Andrea Doria's* crew had long ago winched the liner's anchor chain.

Gary Gentile had been the third diver that morning, after Packer and Gatto. As usual, Gentile had come up with a few pieces of china. Paul Whitttaker and Craig decided they would use their afternoon dive to scout around for the china hole. They went in a few minutes after 2. It took them four minutes to descend to the wreck. Visibility was average: about forty feet. Beyond that, walls of blackness. It was Whittaker's second dive on the ship and he found himself in awe. The anemones and hydroids had taken over, so every surface of the tipped-over liner, where rusty plates of steel did not show through, had a sort of shaggy, meaty look to it, but it was undeniably still a magnificent passenger liner. Long railings and stacked window frames and the S-shaped lifeboat davits—even in the murky depths, the array of geometric shapes together made clear that this was not a pile of rubble, but still vividly a ship, albeit a stricken one. And it did look completely wrong somehow here, at the bottom.

From the anchor line, Whittaker and Craig swam about seventy-five feet toward the ship's stern and dropped into Gimbel's Hole. The two then swam some distance back from the hole. Whittaker began to appreciate the topsy-turvy nature of the wreck, where old decks and ceilings were walls, and old walls were floors and ceilings. None of the once exquisite paneling was left, of course, having long ago been ingested by worms. So the divers proceed deliberately through what effectively are massive steel chutes. It wasn't like any other wreck Whittaker had been on. "You're not worried about getting crammed into a spot that you're not going to get out of," he said. "It's more like getting lost. That's the worry."

The two had been swimming along, with Craig in the lead, when Whittaker realized they had passed the spot that might reveal the china hole. He had kept a wary eye on his depth gauge. The ship rested at 250 feet but the china hole, or at least what they thought was the china hole, was at 210 feet. Working in unfamiliar surroundings, the two men had drifted down to 220. Whittaker, who was diving on air (79 percent nitrogen, 21 percent oxygen), wasn't comfortable with the depth because oxygen can become toxic past 215 feet. He began waving his light back and forth to get Craig's attention. Craig eventually noticed, and Whittaker signaled he was turning around and getting out. Craig agreed, and they made their way out of the wreck. By the time they both pulled themselves back onto the *Seeker*, they had been in the water for almost exactly one hour. Whittaker had planned twenty minutes of bottom time. Craig, breathing Trimix (17 percent oxygen, 35 percent helium and 58 percent nitrogen), had a bit more bottom time—twenty-three minutes.

The two men perspired heavily as they struggled over to the shin-high table that took up about half the *Seeker*'s stern cockpit, where—as was the frequent practice—other divers lifted their tanks from their shoulders. Then Whittaker and Craig tugged off their thick gloves, peeled back their snug-fitting hoods, unzipped their dry suits, and began to step out of their fleece-lined jumpsuits underneath. Both men were also wide-eyed at the haul of china brought up that morning by Gary Gentile.

Gentile brought up another load when he surfaced from his second dive at 6 P.M. Gentile kept generally to himself on the *Seeker*, but no one questioned his skills, his experience, and his instincts. While his prose sometimes bordered on the wacky (the *Andrea Doria* is, Gentile has written, "a beckoning Siren to those whose ears are unwaxed"), it was clear that Gentile was also plainly courageous. If there is a preeminent *Andrea Doria* diver (other than Peter Gimbel, who did it first but who has been dead for several years), Gentile would unquestionably be a candidate for the honor. Maybe he overplays the adventurer-photojournalist role—an author's photo on the back of his self-published *The Technical Diving Handbook* shows him in full hunter's khaki "during a month-long wilderness canoe trip down the George River in Labrador"—but he has also achieved serious victories, such as when he won a permit from the U.S. government in 1989 to dive on the *Monitor*.

On June 23, 1998, he had brought up the most china. It was in the best condition. It was the talk of the boat. His score was highest.

Craig tried to convince Gentile and Dan Crowell to tell him the location of the china trove. He peppered both with questions all evening, and he spoke to John Moyer as well. Moyer was another diving heavyweight, less self-consciously so than either Dan or Gentile, but he wasn't helpful to Craig. Certainly greed drove the senior divers, but they also had a genuine sense that it was safer not to try to explain to Craig how to get to the china hole. Craig had made four dives on the shipwreck. Gentile, Dan, Moyer, and other senior men aboard such as Bart Malone and Steve Gatto had each made more than a hundred dives on the *Andrea Doria*. If they didn't know how best to approach the ship safely, then who did?

At the same time, however, Bart Malone did not approve of Gentile's behavior that day. Malone well understood the craving for china; he had a twenty-by-twenty-four-foot building near his home in Bellmawr, New Jersey, stacked high with *Andrea Doria* loot. No, he didn't exactly sell it, he said. What he meant was, he did not actively, routinely solicit sales. But, he offered cheerily by way of clarification, if you traded him three hundred dollars for a crystal glass etched with ITALIA, well, of course he could do that. Malone was a digger. He found stuff in the muck of the *Andrea Doria* that eluded other people. He wasn't the first guy to find the china hole in any particular year. He was a gifted scavenger. He worked a second-class china cabinet for six straight years in the 1990s. During the 1991 diving season, he bagged more than five hundred pieces from the ship.

So, he acknowledged, he might not have been the right person to sniff at Gentile that day, but he did anyway. He wondered why Gentile did not stow the china to remove it from the gaze of agitated divers such as Craig. It was obvious to Malone that Craig had China Fever, even if he thought the term a stupid one. Craig did not impress Malone as a patient person.

"Hey, Gary, why don't you put this stuff away? It'll psych people out," Malone told Gentile.

Gentile was eating in the *Seeker*'s main cabin. "It's okay, it's okay," he said.

"Gary," Malone continued, "they're fucking beautiful. Gary, you can't leave this stuff here."

Gentile, said Malone, continued to eat.

That night, Craig tried again to get the senior divers to tell him the location of the china hole. He found Gentile and Dan's code for the china hole—"Secret Spot No. 26"—to be condescending. Malone offered to explain how to get to the second-class china cache, but Craig had done enough research to know that this required a three-hundred-foot swim from where the *Seeker*'s anchor line was tied in to the *Andrea Doria*. The long swim meant a lot less time looking for that second-class stuff, and anyway, it wasn't the first class he so fiercely wanted. Gatto tied to convince Craig that when Gary Gentile described the new china hole as a tricky spot, that really meant something. If Gentile deemed it tricky, then it certainly was tricky.

"You want china off the wreck? Be patient," Gatto told Craig. "If you're patient, the dishes will come. Take it easy." With that Gatto walked back inside the main cabin, and Craig studied the *Andrea Doria* deck plans that were posted outside. Someone had said something about the kitchen during the course of the day. Maybe that was the place to go.

The weather degraded the next day. A haze had settled. Surface visibility had cranked down to perhaps two miles. But it was sixty-five degrees and the current moved at less than a mile an hour. The divers at the *Andrea Doria* cared more about current speed than any other measurement of the conditions at the dive site. A fast current would force them to hang on tight to the anchor line during their decompression stops and it could also stir silt on the wreck itself, which could hamper visibility.

Craig was scheduled to dive with Paul Whittaker and Lyn Del Corio. But he wasn't ready to go, or at least it seemed he wasn't ready. So Whittaker and Del Corio went as a two-man team. Whittaker entered the water at 10:26, according to the logs kept by Jenn Samulski. Del Corio followed at 10:27. Craig went in at 10:37, by himself, with his own ideas on the whereabouts of the china hole.

Craig's decision to dive alone did not concern most of those who were aboard the *Seeker*. Diving solo was contrary to a basic rule of recreational scuba diving, which held that people should pair up for safety. But *Andrea Doria* divers are what Himalayan climbers are to weekend hikers. The "rules," which aren't enforced by any law or regulation anyhow, don't apply to these divers. Dan estimates that about 40 percent of the divers enter the water by themselves. The bottom times are short at the *Andrea Doria*—fifteen to twenty minutes maximum—and the divers don't want to be concerned with another diver's safety. Bart Malone called it "big-boy diving," and the big boys did not buddy up. The less experienced divers, however, did work together, and Dan encouraged this even if he did not do it himself. Down on the wreck, Whittaker and Del Corio worked as a team inside the wreck, which they had entered through the big opening everyone called Gimbel's Hole. They found a cache of china. It was a picked-over spot but good enough for them, and they took a few pieces. They took turns holding the light for each other. At some point Whittaker moved a few large panels, and the area in which they were working started to cloud up with billowing silt. Time to go.

Craig saw the white flare of their diving lights as he approached Gimbel's Hole. It was about 10:45 A.M. They all drew together in the darkness there. Whittaker flashed Craig the OK sign with his thumb and index finger. He intended it as a question. Was Craig all right? Craig returned the gesture. He was good. Whittaker then lifted a thumbs-up sign. His dive had gone well. His eyes smiled through his mask. Craig nodded enthusiastically.

Whittaker and Del Corio watched Craig enter Gimbel's Hole. His disappearing form was replaced by a fizzy trail marking his exhalation, but the bubbles burst in moments, vanishing as quickly as chimney smoke wiped away by a hard breeze. Whittaker and Del Corio kicked their fins and headed to the *Seeker*'s anchor line.

Craig dropped into the oval-shaped room that gave the Foyer Deck its name. *Ponte Vestiboli*. He then made a turn toward the *Andrea Doria*'s stern, down a passageway that led to the dining room. The U-shaped dining room straddled the width of the ship, which meant that ninety feet separated the bulwark above Craig's head (this was the wall when the ship rested in its proper orientation) and the bottom of the room— that is, the other original wall. Table legs, long ago bolted to the floor, now jutted from the side like tree branches. Negotiating the dining room is a feat for divers because they must maintain a consistent depth (by monitoring their depth gauge) as they proceed through the sprawling chamber. If they drop down, they could find themselves stumbling upon hallways or companionways they have not memorized from the deck plans. Using time to reorient here eats the clock, as divers already have only fifteen to twenty minutes of bottom time. With five dives to the ship, two of which were surveys outside the hull, Craig had opted for a decidedly problematic penetration.

Somehow Craig made it beyond the dining room to the kitchen. Of course it was a logical place to find china, and he did find some. He dug out three pieces. One was so faded it looked bone white. Two others had rust-colored blotches but bore the unmistakable maroon-and-gold braid that indicated this was first-class china. At the top, capital letters spelled ITALIA and above that hovered the line's classic logo, a red crown.

He stashed the three pieces in the mesh goodie bag clipped to his harness. Then he began to puzzle his exit from the wreck.

Craig's depth gauge showed that in his strenuous effort to bag the china he slipped to a depth of 226 feet. This either happened as he worked his way back to the kitchen or on his return. He had sunk almost fifty feet from when he dropped in the ship through Gimbel's Hole. At some point he got out of the ship, but this had taken some amount of time, and he opted not to ascend the anchor line. If, as was likely, he came out of the ship back through Gimbel's Hole, he would have faced a seventy-foot swim against the current to the anchor line.

Instead, he reached back for his emergency ascent reel—his up line. He tied off the lightweight nylon line to something on the old ship. He then attached a lift bag to the other end and sent it slowly up to the surface. It would act as buoy to let the others know he was ascending on the emergency reel and not on the anchor line.

The lift bag hit the surface at 11:12 A.M. At first, for the *Seeker* crew members, no cause for concern was apparent. Divers sometimes sent their loot ahead of them on lift bags so they wouldn't have to hold on to it as they executed their decompression stops. At the time, thirteen *Seeker* divers were still in the water. The bag could have been anyone's. Steve Gatto had just climbed back on deck after his dive when he and Dan spotted the lift bag flopping in the gray swells. Both men climbed down into the *Seeker*'s Zodiac-style outboard boat and sped over to the lift bag. They pulled it out of the water, but found nothing attached—no bag of goodies. They knew it was Craig's, however, because two laminated tables with decompression stop information were attached. Gatto drew in the line that descended from the bag and found it chafed and almost parted about eighteen inches from the end that had been tied off below.

People did the math in their heads. It said right on the divers' log that Craig planned to be in the water for seventy minutes, including twenty-three minutes on the wreck. If he entered the water at 10:37, and you then added four minutes for the descent, that meant that Craig's bottom time should have run from about 10:41 to 11:01. But the lift bag's appearance on the surface at 11:12 suggested that at perhaps ten minutes after 11 he had been tying off the lift bag when he should have been a solid ten minutes into his series of decompression stops. He was way off schedule. Where was he?

Ten minutes later, at 11:22 A.M., Craig heaved to the surface, facedown. Dan, Gatto, and Moyer had been scanning the surface since the lift bag appeared, and they had no problem picking up Craig's red-and-black dry suit rolling in the water off the *Seeker's* port bow. This time, Gene Peterson bounced over to Craig in the Zodiac with Dan and another diver, Joe Zeisweiss. Peterson climbed out and unclipped Craig's double air tanks, which plummeted more than two hundred feet to the bottom. He rolled Craig on his back. Craig's eyes were bloodshot and he was unresponsive. Blue blotches bloomed on his face. Peterson began mouth-to-mouth resuscitation. Dan and Zeisweiss lifted some of Craig's gear aboard the Zodiac, then hauled Craig aboard.

Craig was on his back on the *Seeker* in a few minutes. A red foam bubbled from the corner of his mouth. A succession of divers emerged from their time underwater unaware of what greeted them on the boat—Tom Packer, Terry Zeller, then Craig's friend Paul Whittaker.

Jim Schultz had not dived that day, and he and John Moyer

cut Craig out of his dry suit. Both men joined in the CPR rounds, along with Peterson and Whittaker and Gatto. They placed an oxygen mask over Craig's mouth while doing chest compressions. The stunned men whispered quiet words of encouragement.

"C'mon, Craig," they said. "C'mon, Craig." But Craig never had vital signs from the moment they got to him in the Zodiac. Even as they attempted to revive him, they called the Coast Guard. Their signal at 11:34 A.M. was garbled, though, so they relayed the information through a passing fishing boat. The call went to the Coast Guard station at Woods Hole, Massachusetts, on Cape Cod. The radio channel finally cleared at 11:51 and Dan was able to relay the situation. The Coast Guard then called Dr. Bruce Gelphia, the on-call physician at the Divers Alert Network, a leading diving-safety organization based at the Duke Medical School in Durham, North Carolina, and Gelphia suggested that Craig be evacuated to Massachusetts General Hospital in Boston. At 12:26, a Coast Guard helicopter was taking off from the air station on Cape Cod, and by 1:00 it had dropped a rescue swimmer near the *Seeker*. He helped secure Craig in the rescue basket.

While the crew and customers of the *Seeker* continued their effort to somehow revive Craig, not everyone could help. Unnoticed, Bart Malone had taken Craig's goodie bag and carried it inside to the *Seeker's* main cabin. He didn't want Craig's prizes disturbed. He examined them. It was obvious where mud had fallen away as they ascended quickly—too quickly—with Craig. From his experience as a digger on the wreck, Malone decided that these pieces had also been concealed in muck when Craig found them. Craig had dug them out. He could also see that the pieces were the kind that more experienced divers had, on occasion, found in the kitchen. There was a dinner plate, an oval serving dish, and a first-class bowl. Malone placed them in the sink.

Later, after Craig had been whisked away by the Coast Guard helicopter, Dan, Gentile, and a few of the other men went inside to rest. Dan wanted everyone to write out statements as soon as they could for the Coast Guard. Best not to leave it for Montauk, because that was an eight-hour ride back. As if in one of their training courses, their discussion focused on re-creating the accident as they thought it might have unfolded. Who saw Craig last? Did anyone know his dive plan? Dan stood up and moved over to the sink. He looked down at Craig's dishes and to no one in particular said: "Where the fuck did he go?"

He took one of the pieces in his hand. "Well," he said, "I know where he got this one from." He looked over at Gentile.

"Yeah," Gentile said, "he got it from the kitchen."

A hush fell. The men eyed each other. Streams of emotion ran through Jim Schultz. He was happy for Craig that he had achieved his goal on the wreck, yet angry and pained that Craig's thinking process had been seized up with plain greed. Wasn't Craig smarter than that? They had dived together for several years, and they had a schtick they did when deciding whether to go ahead with a dangerous penetration on one of the wrecks close to Jersey.

"That's not worth it to me!" Schultz would say.

"It's worth it to me!" Craig would say.

The crew got the *Seeker* under way at ten minutes after one, just a few minutes after they watched the Coast Guard helicopter thunder north into the haze, to Boston. A doctor at the medical examiner's office there pronounced Craig dead at 2:09 P.M., moments after he was wheeled inside Massachusetts General. Dr. Stanton Kessler concluded that the cause of death was "drowning and barotrauma due to rapid ascent in salt water."

Craig had rocketed to the surface so fast that his bloodstream had flooded with nitrogen bubbles. An autopsy had also shown that Craig had an enlarged heart; Kessler told the Coast Guard that the condition of the Craig's heart could not be ruled out as a contributing factor in his death.

As one of the Long Beach Island contingent aboard the *Seeker*, Schultz helped organize Craig's stuff to take home. Everyone talked about the fact that Craig had made it out of the wreck and managed to send up the lift bag. He had escaped from some trouble inside the wreck and had gotten out. Gene Peterson examined Craig's nylon up line. Its end was apparently worn through. The rope now measured about 150 feet. Some of the divers wondered if Craig had tied the line off, only to have it get caught somewhere on the wreck and sawed through. Craig had apparently been in a hurry. One of his knives was missing. What had he used the knife for? No one knew. Gary Gentile, who had almost twenty years on some of the divers, said some thoughtful words about the risky nature of deep diving. But as Jim Schultz packed his dead friend's things, his mind framed the situation in a less noble way. "Fuck! Why was it worth it? Why?"

That afternoon, the telephone rang upstairs in the investigations department at the Coast Guard station in New Haven, Connecticut. It was Providence calling.

Lieutenant Lisa Campbell, an investigator with the Coast Guard in Providence, Rhode Island, had a favor to ask. The wreck site of the *Andrea Doria* fell within the geographic jurisdiction of her unit, but the *Seeker* was already under way to Montauk, which was in New Haven's jurisdiction. Could the Marine Safety Office in New Haven send someone to meet the boat? Lieutenant Timothy Dickerson, the thirty-two-year-old assistant chief in the investigations department, dispatched Eric Allen, a petty officer assigned to the Coast Guard in Coram, Long Island.

Dickerson had no plans to lead the investigation. He was backlogged as usual typing up voluminous reports on local sinkings, safety inspections, groundings, and drownings.

He was a tall man, bespectacled, with a boyish, banged haircut. He was a whiz in mathematics and thought he might become a math teacher when he got out of the service in a couple of years. If he stood at the window of his office, he could just make out the permanent chains of traffic pulling along Interstate 95, the freeway linking New York City and New England, but his view also took in Long Island Sound. The Marine Safety Office where he worked was in a constant bustle with small spills from oil tankers, the occasional stranded lobster boat, countless inspections along the North and South Shores of Long Island Sound, from New Haven to Mattituck, New York. A novice diver who had strapped on a single tank once while on vacation in the Caribbean, Dickerson had no intention of probing the death of Craig Sicola or any other diver at the *Andrea Doria*.

When he heard that Craig had dived by himself, he cringed.

Why hadn't this guy dived with a buddy, he asked himself. Doesn't everyone?

Dickerson knew nothing at all about how things worked at the *Andrea Doria.*

On Long Beach Island, the little telephone call played over in Karen Moscufo's head as she lay awake at 5 A.M.

"Hi Mom. I'm coming home," Chris said.

"Why? I thought you were sleeping over at your friend's."

"I'm coming home, Mom."

He came home and told her about Craig. People streamed over to her house. She went to bed far past midnight and woke up at 5. She was angry and had something she wanted to do.

She walked outside and down to the beach and turned toward Craig's house. It was eighteen blocks. The sun was just rising, compressing the streaks on the horizon into a thin blue band, and the sand felt cool under her feet. Karen felt like a widow for the second time, though she and Craig were not married. As she walked, a friend parked at the beach and got out of his pickup; he had been thinking of Craig, too. He asked if she was all right. Something about that chance encounter sapped her anger. She still had a key to Craig's place, and let herself in. She went straight into the living room. Craig displayed a framed, blow-up copy of the *Andrea Doria* deck plans there. Her original idea was to take them off the wall and smash them.

Instead, she unhooked them gently from the wall and set them on the table and, with her index finger, traced through the maze where she believed Craig had gone, places Craig had told her about. Her long, blond hair fell upon the glass. She imagined him getting his china. She was glad that he had gotten his china, but her anger started to fizz inside her again.

Why couldn't he just wait and explore the ship safely, she wondered. He was such a child, and obviously hadn't given much thought at all to the repercussions of his stupid death. "You didn't come up alive," she said aloud, "but your china did."

She walked to his room, and over to his closet. With her slender fingers, she touched Craig's clothes hanging there in the early-morning light. She breathed in deeply so she could smell him.

Five days passed before Craig's funeral. The mourners filed out of St. Thomas of Villanova Church in Surf City and headed toward the ocean. They gathered in a circle on the sand and placed one of Craig's longboards in the middle. Someone had found it leaning up against his house, where someone else had scrawled WE LOVE YOU, CRAIG on it. Everyone in the circle had a flower in his or her hand. People took turns saying a few words, then they each dropped their flowers on the surfboard. Then about thirty of Craig's friends paddled through the breakers to the calm flats 150 yards out. They formed a circle there and sat straight up on their boards, as if they were waiting for the next set. They grabbed each other's hands. Someone pushed Craig's surfboard, now piled with flowers from the ceremony on the beach, into the center of the surfers' circle. They started yelling thing like, "Craig, we love you!" You could hear them from the beach.

Louis Sicola lowered himself into a sea kayak with another paddler. He wore a life jacket and a lei. They cut through the surf and into the middle of the circle out there, next to Craig's board. "Craig, we love you!" It was like a Quaker meeting, as people yelled things haphazardly. It was a good place to shout out the name of Craig Sicola. He was a surfer, after all. Out on the flats, just beyond the breakers, is where he sometimes waited on the water, surveying the potential, really, as the swells rolled under his board and tickled his feet, right before he would paddle furiously after the rising curl to catch a porcelain wave, fired in the glow of the morning.

Someone flipped Craig's board. The underside glistened in the sunshine, and the flowers colored the water for a minute before the ocean began to take them under, one by one.

Four

At age sixty, Lee Somers, a professor at the University of Michigan, was a gray eminence in the fields of oceanography, marine geology, and scuba diving. He had published for three decades on the development of undersea laboratories and diving safety. The state of Michigan asked Somers to analyze commercial and recreational diving deaths, and the U.S. government asked him to review the diving manual used by the National Oceanic and Atmospheric Administration. Although his deep-diving days were behind him, Somers kept wired to scuba's electronic grapevine. Here, in the late 1990s, divers used a growing number of websites to trade vacation ideas, dispense advice on the exploration of shipwrecks, and offer withering reviews of the hot new gear. Sometimes, Somers's computer screen even flickered with real news.

"*Andrea Doria* gets another one," said one in a flurry of postings in a chatroom from the rec.scuba site. It was the last week of June. Craig Sicola had drowned a few days earlier on his *Seeker* charter to the *Andrea Doria*. Craig's death had not reached the media in the Midwest. Even in the East, Craig's death had made only small headlines. The Coast Guard had not even issued a statement. This was the first Lee Somers had heard of it.

"Anyone have details?" another post read.

There was only one person Somers had to call: Richard Roost, Jr.

Richard owned a strip-mall scuba shop in Ann Arbor—the only dive shop in the college town thirty-five miles west of Detroit. A heavy-shouldered man with a walrus mustache, Richard, forty-six, was a former auto mechanic who had taken up diving after he tried it on vacation in the Bahamas. He quickly decided that scuba diving, not fixing engines, would be his career. In 1985, he paid thirty-eight thousand dollars for Divers, Inc., the scuba business across from the Goodyear garage where he worked. Eventually he opened a second shop in nearby Novi.

He soon emerged as a major force in the Great Lakes scuba community. He trained police and firefighter diving teams and, for fun, swam with sharks in the Bahamas wearing a suit knit of high-tech mail. Somers, the academic, and Richard, the blue-collar diver who had wriggled around all the key shipwrecks in the clear lake waters off the thumb of northern Michigan, started a dive-safety road show. Their last presentation had been before the Ford Seahorses, the scuba club for employees at the auto plant in nearby Dearborn. Richard always reminded Somers to promote "continuing education"; not only would that advance the culture of safety in which they both believed, it would also advance the cause everywhere of diving instructors such as Richard Roost. That was Richard's sense of humor. Low key, all the way.

Richard hung up the telephone and relayed the news to Scott Campbell, the husky thirty-one-year-old former marine who helped him manage Divers, Inc. Richard did not seem shaken by the news, even though he was scheduled to meet the *Seeker* in Montauk in a few days, for his own ride out to the wreck of the *Andrea Doria*. But then, Richard could be difficult to read.

Richard was private and meticulous, a man given to long periods of silence, often in the presence of others. He cultivated numerous relationships in the diving and law enforcement communities throughout Michigan, yet few of his friends had ever been to his house. He lived alone. He was divorced from Cyndee Roost, a nurse he had introduced to scuba. They had dived under the ice together in Lake Michigan, tethered with safety ropes to each other, and even after the divorce, they kept in almost daily contact. He devoted hours to tinkering wordlessly with his equipment in the basement of his Ann Arbor store, which he called, with mock gravity, "Dive Central."

He had been a slightly odd all-American boy. He was an Eagle Scout at the young age of twelve, and a state-champion archer, but his aunt also recalled him often standing at her back screen door, when he visited her farm in the summer, staring wordlessly across the fields. On a long-ago family trip to the Civil War battlefield at Gettsyburg, Pennsylvania, young Richard had taken picture after picture of the soldiers' tombstones. He had hundreds of such photographs. When he was twenty-nine years old, he had a will drafted that instructed his heirs that "an above-ground grave marker of not less than twenty-four (24) inches in height" be erected within six months of his death. Later in life, his apparently natural melancholy deepened with the death of his twin sister, Rebecca, at the age of forty-four from breast cancer.

For his public audience, Richard had a serious presentation: He showed up at diving shows in jacket and tie while the others wore their T-shirts imprinted with images of their boats, or shop logo, and blue jeans. His closest friends, of course, knew the warmer dimension of his personality. Some knew he had proposed to Cyndee on a romantic diving trip they had taken to Bali. Others treasured vacation snapshots from Fiji, when Richard, deadpan expression on his face, modeled the goofy hats he had crafted from palm fronds. He also slapped stickers of mermaids on all his diving tanks, which always came as a surprise for those who had met the bearish, reserved businessman from Michigan. He had fun with the surprise. On a diver-information sheet Dan Crowell handed out on his charter trips, where it asked for religion, Richard wrote, "Any."

The news about Craig Sicola did not appear to faze Richard. He would not offer the contrast, but others did: There was no comparison between Craig Sicola and Richard Roost. Craig had dived for ten years on and off, for fun. Richard had dived for twenty-five years professionally. True, Craig had crucial experience in the murky cold-water wrecks of the Northeast, and had even dived previously on the *Andrea Doria*, but Richard trained police officers to pull out drivers who had plunged their cars under ice. He knew bad conditions. In a sport where many people claimed to be expert at "skip breathing," few divers seemed to get more bottom time out of a tank of air than Richard. His scuba rig was streamlined, his gear of the highest quality, and he serviced the stuff himself. He moved underwater with intelligence and calm. In Michigan, they called Richard Roost "Scuba God."

Richard was determined to visit the *Andrea Doria* and bring back first-class china as proof. He planned to videotape the sunken liner and post the images on his shops' website. By the time Lee Somers contacted him, he had already packed for his trip to Montauk. He had even picked out a new mask—black with a lime-green strap. The year before, bad weather had forced the cancellation of an *Andrea Doria* trip he had booked on the *Seeker*. Dan had mailed him a copy of the deck plans, and over the winter Richard had studied the plans faithfully. He knew that memorizing the relevant layouts—in particular, the ship's Foyer Deck—would be one more way to increase his margin for safety. "Plan your dive and dive your plan." He had said it many times to more than two thousand divers he had personally trained. He practiced what he preached. Although he planned to make the drive to New York alone, he shared his enthusiasm for the trip with everyone. One day, after leading a training session with the Washtenaw County Sheriff's Department at a local college, he relaxed at poolside with his friend Deputy David Egeler.

"When I dive the *Doria*," he told Egeler that day, "my life will be complete."

It took fourteen hours to drive from the Detroit area to Montauk, and by the time Richard arrived at the Star Island Yacht Club, the summer night had unfurled a velvety sky glittering with stars. Dan had a weather-fax machine in the *Seeker's* wheelhouse, and the reports burping out were discouraging. Although it was a windless evening on the east end of Long Island, the skies were stormy over the *Andrea Doria* wreck site. Dan scrubbed the charter.

Undeterred, Richard signed up for a trip a week later, after the July 4 holiday weekend. He climbed back into his Divers, Inc., van and headed home to Michigan.

Dan did not like to cancel *Andrea Doria* charters. His customers were paying close to a thousand dollars for a few days' diving, and he also loved diving the site himself. So he seized on the next weather envelope, which was just a couple of days after Richard Roost had left for Michigan. One of his regular customers, a Hackensack, New Jersey, attorney named Bill Cleary, had organized an *Andrea Doria* charter. Among the customers was Vince Napoliello, thirty-two, a financial adviser who was from north Jersey but who lived in Brooklyn. Affable, handsome, funny, Vince was a regular *Seeker* diver who, after several years of busy Northeast wreck diving, had decided to back away from the sport. He and his fiancée, Marisa Gengaro, were to be married the next spring, and she was not comfortable about the diving.

Vince's career at Legg Mason in the financial district was also heating up, with the roaring stock market of the late 1990s providing tremendous opportunities for young, energetic investment advisers like him.

He would still enjoy the water—he would keep the speedboat named *Champagne*—but technical diving was time consuming if it was to be done well, and he had less time now. He had agreed to go on Bill Cleary's trip, though. Cleary had called him repeatedly at the office, where Vince's screensaver depicted a swimming shark. They had discussed the death of Craig Sicola only ten days earlier and had agreed, as had many in the Northeast diving community, that Craig had been too aggressive. What was he doing in the kitchen anyhow? They never thought to blame Dan Crowell or any member of the *Seeker* crew. They held to the code among divers of their level, that once a diver enters the water, he's responsible for himself. Divers such as Cleary and Vince Napoliello also felt honored to dive off the *Seeker*.

"If you look at the typical *Seeker* dive," Cleary said, "you have guys like John Moyer, who owns the salvage rights to the *Andrea Doria,* and guys like John Chatterton, who owns the salvage rights to the *Carolina.* You have Gary Gentile, the author of more than twenty books on diving. These are the guys you want to be around. No matter how many people die on the *Seeker*, it's still the best dive boat in the Northeast."

On July 5, Cleary and Vince worked as a team at the *Doria*. This is how many of the best divers work. One holds lights while the other man digs carefully through the silt for china, or works on bolts holding a porthole in place, or they cut each other out of the fishing lines clinging to the wreck. Cleary and Vince had agreed to a dive with seventeen minutes of bottom time at the wreck, but they had not counted on taking fifteen minutes to get to the china hole they had targeted. It was hard to predict such things; a stronger current at the wreck or bad visibility there could slow the divers down. So they worked the hole quickly, lifting twenty pieces of china before leaving. For them, staying longer was not an option they would seriously consider. Time management is a cornerstone of deep-diving safety, and both men were proficient, prudent divers. They bagged lead-crystal salad bowls and cups, including some of the prized "Oriental" design. On the deck of the *Seeker* later, they gave each other hard high-fives. It was an experience worth celebrating. They had worked fast inside the wreck, executed a safe ascent, and taken a haul of china from the *Andrea Doria*. Until that moment, Vince had been noncommittal about whether to dive on the *Andrea Doria* again. But that afternoon, laughing in the sun on the deck of the *Seeker*, he said of course he'd go one more time with Cleary. The date of the charter was August 4. After that, he told the others, no more.

As Vince drove west from Montauk on July 6, headed home to Brooklyn, Richard Roost once again drove east. He puffed on a cigar he had just bought in East Hampton. He drove on the two-lane Montauk Highway, first where it is shaded by heavy oaks and maples in East Hampton and Amagansett, then where it flattens out astride the dunes shouldered against the Atlantic Ocean, and finally where the road plunges back into the trees above Montauk, into impenetrable choking waves of greenery that drag the pavement into shadow before suddenly descending, with a suddenness that takes people's breath away, to reveal the hook-shaped outline of Montauk Point.

Richard and Scott Campbell had a running gag. Whoever was on vacation would call the other man and say what a great time he was having and how excellent the weather was, even if it was untrue. Richard told Campbell he had just picked up cigars and was on the last leg of the long drive. Campbell heard a lightness in Richard's voice. Others back home had noticed it, too. He had been telling people that, after he dived on the *Andrea Doria*, he wanted to play more, cut back on the insanity of his schedule with Divers, Inc., the hours running the shop, the hours afterward leading training courses, the considerable time he poured into training the police and fire divers. He had hinted to some who knew him that the death of his sister had prompted him to reevaluate his life. He wanted to make progress on the list of life goals he had shared with his father. He wanted to see the Pyramids in Egypt, hike the Great Wall in

China, and dive on the *Andrea Doria*. And here he was, about to dive on the great liner.

Richard's life was a string of accomplishments achieved with gritty determination. He pumped gas in high school to get the Camaro he craved. He learned to dive and became an expert. He bought the shop, and he made the passage from working for hourly mechanic's wages to unlocking the doors of his own small business each morning, and pulling on a coat and tie to attend out-of-town industry conventions. His happy tone of voice was justified. He was crossing something off the list.

Campbell ended the conversation with another running joke the two men shared. The banter was rooted in Campbell's covetousness about Richard's collection of antique diving gear, including several heavy, old helmets.

Campbell: "If you don't come back, can I have the Mark V helmet?"

Richard: "Sure!"

When Richard pulled into the lot at the Star Island Yacht Club that night, he learned that he was the only diver on the charter who did not know any of the other customers. Dan's crew included some of the familiar faces: Moyer, Gentile, and, of course, Jenn Samulski. Several of the customers had law enforcement or military backgrounds, which was typical of many *Seeker* divers. Richard had also served in the Army in the mid-1970s, stationed in stateside bases. Robert Ryan was a captain in the police department in Brick, the New Jersey town where Dan and Jenn lived, and Joseph Gaddy, a computer systems expert, had served on nuclear submarines in the U.S. Navy.

Gaddy had been also Dan's diving student. Dan spent part of every winter leading classes in the room off the garage in the house in Brick. Dan planned to use Gaddy's dives on the *Andrea Doria* as "checkout" dives for Gaddy's certification to use Trimix breathing gases. Dan had a policy that anyone who rode the *Seeker* out to the *Andrea Doria* already had to be Trimix certified, or to be a Trimix student accompanied by his or her instructor. You couldn't earn a more advanced open-water certification than Trimix, and Dan used the achievement as a qualification for anyone who wanted to dive off his boat. The certification meant the diver had a specific number of deep dives while using the Trimix.

Dan, however, did not believe in rules for rules' sake, and he made routine exceptions to his Trimix rule. For one thing, he was Gaddy's instructor, and he made no plans to accompany Gaddy on any of his checkout dives. Some of his most trusted crew members, whose experience dated back before Trimix certifications were even marketed to the diving community, were also not held to the Trimix requirement. Dan judged them expert divers, and no one who knew these divers' exploits could argue. Students such as Gaddy also were sometimes made exceptions, often with another diving instructor vouching for the diver in question. While Dan respected the training provided by the certification agencies—he taught some of their programs—he placed deeper faith in the judgment of his fellow big-boy divers. Dan said that a dive on the *Andrea Doria* was about the best place a student could practice the techniques involved in Trimix diving.

Not everyone agreed. The most vocal opponent was Steve Bielenda, master of the *Wahoo*, who reasoned that the *Andrea*

Doria's remoteness from emergency medical care made it inadvisable as a site on which to conduct what the industry called "check-out dives." Dan, however, could dismiss Bielenda's objections as rantings of a rival. Still, some of Dan Crowell's friends also disagreed with him on this point. In particular, diver John Moyer said publicly that the *Doria* was not the place for training.

Joel Silverstein felt the same way. Silverstein had almost fifty dives on the *Andrea Doria* and had built a career in the development of diving-course materials and even diving equipment designed specifically for technical divers. For a while he had published an issue-oriented diving magazine that, unlike the perception that many divers held about other scuba magazines, contained more than photographs of tropical fish and advertisements for Cozumel travel packages. He felt Trimix students needed a more controlled training environment. There, they could build their skills without balancing the goal of lifting china from the famous shipwreck. But in the politics of the Northeast diving tribe, Silverstein's view could be minimized. He was a longtime friend of Bielenda's who long ago had chosen the *Wahoo* camp, even if Dan and Silverstein had no particular personal animosity between them. Joel Silverstein was a *Wahoo* guy.

In an industry that regulated itself, opinions about what constitutes safe procedures counted as much as formal policies. There were no laws about such things. People such as Dan Crowell depended on the independent nature of their sport. Surely, someone not qualified wouldn't be stupid enough to come all the way out here and dive, right?

Richard Roost had faxed Dan his Trimix certification from the International Association of Nitrox & Technical Divers.

IANTD was the agency headed by legendary diver Tom Mount and Trimix pioneer Billy Deans. He also displayed the certificate at his diving shop in Ann Arbor. It proclaimed Richard a "Trimix Diver" and was dated September 14, 1997.

Dan divided the divers who trudged aboard his boat as either "scary" or not. Some of the customer-divers were obviously scary. They were flabby. Their equipment looked dried out or, on rare occasions, rusty. They got into a rush on their dives because they didn't keep an eye on the time. Their gear was arranged sloppily. They deviated from their stated dive plan. They failed to file a dive plan with Jenn.

He had decided right away that Richard was not scary. Dan was impressed that Richard had two diving shops, and had trained other divers for years, and he was also comforted by Richard's laid-back but serious demeanor. In conversations, it became clear that Richard had studied the *Andrea Doria* deck plans he had sent him (so Dan's time had not been wasted, and Dan liked this) and had researched the depths of the various decks on his own. Richard's gear gleamed; much was new, and what was not new had been maintained with care. He noticed that Richard lugged a laptop computer aboard the *Seeker*. That wasn't unusual because a lot of divers were using new software products to work out decompression schedules, which varied with the Trimix blend they used. In Dan's eyes, what distinguished Richard was that he also brought along a color printer.

The *Seeker* left Montauk that night around 11 and made the hundred miles to the wreck by dawn. Richard struck the others divers as extremely reserved. His relative silence may also have been due to exhaustion. He had driven from Michigan to New York and had now endured an eight-hour steam from Montauk to the *Andrea Doria*. And for all his love of shipwrecks, Richard did not much like boats. He was seasick. He had some over-the-counter seasickness remedies with him, though it wasn't clear that he had taken the pills. He exhibited the tendencies of someone not entirely comfortable with the boat's rocking motion. More often than not, he could be found in the cabin, resting.

The atmosphere at the wreck site was different from the days when Craig Sicola and the others had visited ten days earlier. First, another boat was also anchored there. It was the *Wahoo*—or RV *Wahoo*, for "Research Vessel," as its owner Bielenda liked to call it. Bielenda and Dan had said many harsh words about each other, but their relationship was now in a tentative phase of mutual toleration.

For years, Bielenda's boat was the indisputable top charter to the *Andrea Doria*. The *Wahoo* was the able platform for John Moyer's complex expedition to remove seven-hundred-pound ceramic friezes from the *Doria*'s Winter Garden, although it had been a *Seeker* team (which included some of the same divers who worked with Moyer) that had secured what Gary Gentile called the "ultimate artifact," the ship's auxiliary bell. By the late 1990s, the *Seeker* was operating triple the number of *Andrea Doria* diving charters. It was clearly the No. 1 boat. Some of Bielenda's former customers (such as Gary Gentile) now crewed with Dan.

When Richard Roost awoke in the early hours of July 7, a ceiling of clouds hung only a hundred feet above the boat. The sun was low on the blur that marked the horizon, a white disc in the mist. The men's bare arms glistened with the sticky sea air, and tendrils of fog even reached down and coiled around the *Seeker*'s communications mast.

The pewter-colored sea was flat, however, and this was the most important weather factor at hand. Those on the *Seeker* would not be bounced too much on the surface, and divers inching back up the anchor line on their long decompression would not have to struggle to stay on the line. Dan was eager for the trip to go well, so he could put the dispiriting Sicola death behind him and lead the rest of the summer's charters. He had even considered quitting the business, and at first felt he shared in the blame for Craig's death. He wondered if he could advance his ambition to become an underwater videographer by simply diving off other people's boats. Craig Sicola had been such a likable, gung-ho personality, known to many south Jersey divers, that his death came like a plate crashing down at a restaurant. Divers were stunned. Then, like customers turning back to their meals as waiters swept up the mess, they quickly returned to *Andrea Doria*. Except for the one trip scrubbed by weather, the *Seeker* did not cancel a single charter. Called by a couple of reporters in the Northeast, Dan described himself as "simply the bus driver" to the *Doria*. He could not control everything that occurred to those on the bus, he said.

This time, Dan had a group of savvy divers aboard, all of whom he knew well, except for Richard Roost. He had feared Richard might be what Northeast divers derided as a "quarry diver"—someone used to exploring featureless, vertical shafts but with little understanding of wreck penetration or ocean currents. A few minutes' conversation, however, had established that Richard had poked inside of wrecks from Lake Michigan to Truk Lagoon. He wasn't scary at all.

In his customary morning safety briefing, and despite his general confidence about the group aboard, Dan strongly encouraged Richard and two other first-timers to the wreck— Ryan and Gaddy—not to go inside the ship until they had first oriented themselves on the outside of the hull. No one voiced an objection. Dan suggested they make their first dive an exploratory swim along the ship's Promenade Deck.

When the *Andrea Doria* was still afloat, the main feature of the Promenade Deck had been its wide, teak-floored walkway lined with a deck-to-ceiling wall of windows often open to the sea air. The three-hundred-foot expanse of glass was long gone now, with barnacles whitening the geometric skeleton of the window frames. Dan recommended a survey of this deck in part because the *Seeker's* anchor line was shackled there, midway between the ship's bow and stern. All the divers had to do was descend the anchor line and they would be in perfect position to proceed with the dive.

Richard went in first, at 10:27 A.M. Gaddy followed at 10:29 and Ryan at 10:30. In minutes they were creeping along the Promenade Deck of the mammoth wreck. The hull of the ship is paved with crustaceans and fist-sized snails, with eight-inch-long anemones waving in the current like fields of poppies bending in the breeze.

Gaddy spied a set of double doors and slowed to lower himself feetfirst into the opening, then push himself up and out. He had done exactly what Dan had asked him not to on the first dive. Maybe, Gaddy thought, what he did had not really counted as a penetration. Richard did not enter the ship. Ryan noticed that Richard moved smoothly underwater. He did not stir much silt at all as he kicked along the ship, almost as if he hadn't really passed by. He seemed instinctively to know exactly how much distance to place between his body and the wreck. Richard would not push the boundaries on this first dive.

Doria divers try to get in two dives per day on their charter trips. Between dives, they must wait hours to off-gas the Trimix they breathe—by exhaling—so their tissues can normalize. Usually, a four-hour interval suffices. Divers try to sleep between dives if they can. As Jolie Bookspan, of the Undersea and Hyperbaric Medical Society, has written, diving physiologists believe that overexertion may be linked to cases of decompression sickness. It's not clear whether exhaustion somehow skews the decompression process by placing a biological demand on divers to spend more time decompressing than their tables would indicate. It may simply spur muddled decision making, as in any sport.

Richard rested, but did not sleep between dives on the first day. He tinkered quietly with his air tanks. He tapped on the keys of his laptop. He also chatted with a few of the customers. He told Dave Alderson that on one of his upcoming dives, he wanted to see the *Doria*'s three swimming pools, which were near the ship's stern.

He also spent a lot of time staring at Dan Crowell and Gary Gentile, who were using toothbrushes to clean the little cache of china they had brought up on their morning dives.

Richard maintained his conservative approach on his second dive that day. He and Gaddy swam to the ship's stern and hovered there by the great liner's nineteen-foot-tall propellers, once shiny and smooth and now mushy with boggy layers of marine life.

A bright sunny sky greeted the divers the next morning, a welcome change from the clouds of the first day. Richard planned to change his approach to the *Andrea Doria*. He had not worked his way to the *Doria* to remain content to swim along the wreck's exterior.

He was pointed down the anchor line by 7:59 A.M. In five minutes he was on the ship and in another few minutes, he had located the china closet inside the ship that had been located two weeks earlier by Gary Gentile. He accomplished the feat with no obnoxious haranguing of the crew; he had studied the deck plans and had remembered. He grabbed one cup and three saucers, each bearing the maroon-and-gold braid that identified it as first-class china. Richard carefully traced his steps back out of the ship, swam again along the Promenade Deck, and entered the ship a second time. As he moved inside, he frequently checked landmarks and objects inside that he could use to guide himself back out. On that clear day, rays of dying sunlight reached like silver knives into the water and, much deeper, inside the darkened Promenade, Richard saw the ambient light as a series of windows stained with glowing blue light. He was mesmerized and comforted. Here he was in the dark, at last having summited the Everest of his life's vocation, gazing hushed at the sapphire portals to the Atlantic Ocean. There were so many ways to get out fast, if he needed to.

After climbing back aboard the *Seeker*, he showed Dan his china. The pieces were painted with coppery stains where they had been stuck in the silt, just like the prizes brought up by Dan and Gentile. Dan was surprised that Richard had retrieved china on his own, surprised that Richard had even penetrated the ship. Richard told him that the dive had been easier than he had expected. He saw that there were many ways to move in and out of the Promenade Deck in particular.

"You can see all the portholes," Richard told Dan. "You can see all the doorways. It's not like you can get lost in there."

"Uh, yeah," Dan said. That was it exactly. If you had a cool head about things, nothing would go wrong. You just had to study up beforehand and know where you were on the wreck as you dived it. He had nothing to worry about with this guy.

"I mean, Jesus," Richard said, "I thought it was going to be the dive from hell."

Richard was the first diver in the water in the afternoon. He went in at 1:02 P.M. Three hours and forty-two minutes had passed since he emerged from his morning dive; he hadn't quite waited the four-hour interval between dives that he had planned. None of the other divers that day had failed to wait their entire interval between dives. It wasn't unusual to cut the intervals short a few minutes, although with a fatigued diver, or one not feeling well, it was not a good idea. Few divers would describe such an action as reckless, but neither was it the safest possible approach at one of the world's most challenging dives.

A diver named Steve Berman lifted himself up to the *Seeker* at 2:38 P.M. He mentioned that was he was surprised that he had not seen Richard on the way back up the anchor line. The two men had dived alone, but within ten minutes of each other. It made sense that they would encounter each other at the end of their dives, one above the other during their decompression stops. On one of Jenn Samulski's sheets that charted the divers' day, the one titled "Dive Plan," she had marked Richard's total run time for his

July 8 dives as eighty minutes. He went in at 1:02, so that meant he expected to be back on the deck of the *Seeker* deck at 2:20.

He was late.

It was possible that he had miscalculated the amount of decompression he would require. But this was a professional diver, and he had been crunching decompression tables on his computer aboard the *Seeker*. In Richard's case, such an error seemed unlikely. At 2:43, Jenn made a note to herself: "Diver Richard Roost 20 mins overdue."

Four minutes later, she radioed the skipper of the *Wahoo*, Janet Bieser. Did the *Wahoo* have anyone hanging on its anchor line?

It was possible, the *Seeker* crew reasoned, that a newcomer to the *Andrea Doria* such as Richard would ascend the wrong anchor line and surface at the wrong dive boat. It was not a common mistake, but it did happen, and when it did, the mistaken diver received heaps of verbal abuse from the others on the charter. The *Wahoo* crew were fairly certain that the two men hanging on their line were their divers, but would confirm that once they surfaced, and radio back to the *Seeker*.

Only two divers, Dan Crowell and Steve Brozyna, were still diving on the wreck as Jenn and the rest of those aboard the *Seeker* realized the growing seriousness of the situation. Bob Ryan had been preparing for an afternoon dive. Instead, he offered to stay topside and help. His written statement to the Coast Guard reflected both his police training and the self-conscious, quasi-military atmosphere that settled on the *Seeker* when one of its divers was in trouble. "I unsuited," he wrote, "and took up a visual observation point on the wheel house level of the *Seeker* and scanned the surrounding waters with field glasses."

No one due to go in the water that afternoon wanted to dive for fun now. They began to expect the worst. They worked together so, if at all possible, they would not go home without the body of Richard Roost. Although they were recreational divers, they each had trained to an elite level and thus gained entry to a sort of brotherhood. It mattered little that this was merely a bond in sport, so when it became clear someone in the brotherhood had died, they acted as soldiers in the field or fire-fighters on the job. To them, it felt wrong to do less than the utmost to get Richard back aboard the boat. Customers watched the water from spots at the bow and along the boat's rails. They were looking for an inflated bag to break the surface, which could be towing Richard's goodie bag or the top end of his Jersey line. Maybe he was decompressing on the Jersey line, as Craig Sicola had apparently tried.

At 3:20, Janet Bieser called Jenn and told her she had sent an underwater slate down to the divers hanging on that boat's anchor line, asking them to confirm who they were. They were *Wahoo* divers.

Minutes later, John Moyer unhooked the marine-band radio and tried to contact the Coast Guard. He couldn't establish con-tact, though. Maybe yesterday's weather had shifted north, in between the *Seeker* and Cape Cod, where the Coast Guard had a boat station at Woods Hole and helicopters at a nearby air base.

Dan came out of the water at 3:47. He reacted to the news with anger, recognition of the inevitability of what was hap-pening, resignation and more rage. He did the math: If Richard had entered the water at 1:02 and it was now almost four, he almost certainly was dead. The longest run time of any dive on the trip had been two hours. Richard, who had planned to be underwater for only eighty minutes, had now been gone three hours. Even if he had surfaced safely, he was nowhere to be seen.

In retrospect, Dan could understand why Craig Sicola had gotten into trouble, but how could Richard Roost? He had made a deep penetration of the *Andrea Doria* on only his third dive ever to the wreck. As he snapped his neoprene hood off his head and slicked back his perspiration-soaked hair, Dan began to seethe. Again, he'd be forced to explain what happened to a collection of people who had no true appreciation for how diving operations worked at the *Doria*. They just didn't know.

He'd have to deal with the Coast Guard investigators, maybe even Lieutenant Tim Dickerson, whom he considered professionally unfit to probe a deep-diving accident and a bureaucratic dweeb to boot. Dickerson actually thought *Andrea Doria* divers should always dive together! Reporters might be at the dock; they certainly would call his listed telephone number or e-mail him. They knew even less than Dickerson. And Roost's family. Did he have kids? They had to find the body. More idiotic flames would flash on the scuba Internet chatrooms, labeling his famous boat "the morgue boat" or "the evil death boat." Dan believed he had a tough job. He balanced egos on the *Seeker*, tried to keep everyone happy, or at least respectful toward one another, even if he could not control the social grouping that just happened aboard, usually the crew off by itself and the paying customers forming their own temporary relationships.

This was the worst feeling he could imagine: climbing back on the deck of the *Seeker* and being told that one of his divers was missing.

There just weren't many people who did this kind of diving. He sensed a kinship with Richard Roost, felt he understood why Richard needed to be at the *Andrea Doria*. Dan's good feeling about the trip and even the summer began to slip away, not all at once, but through the afternoon, bit by bit, like clods of earth skipping down a steep bluff.

Despite the frustrations churning inside, Dan remained reasonably calm on the surface. His exchanges with others now came in abbreviated orders and responses. That was all the evidence the others had that Dan had been rocked hard by the unfolding events. Ryan, the police captain who headed his 112-officer department's investigative division, describes Dan as a "subtle personality" who will not exhibit "gross changes" no matter the situation. Dan threw his energies into finding Richard. He climbed the stairs to the wheelhouse. He sketched out a search plan. He asked for volunteers and got them easily. Anyone who could go, who had waited long enough since the last dive, wanted to help. They weren't leaving anyone out here.

The *Wahoo* radioed over. Their two divers entering the water would keep an eye out for Richard down below. One said he planned to go to the ship's kitchen, a possible destination for Richard because it contained an accessible store of china (with his morning dive, Richard had shown considerable confidence in his ability to explore the ship). John Moyer finally got a strong signal to the Coast Guard, to the station at Woods Hole, on Cape Cod. He relayed the *Seeker*'s position and the situation.

The Coast Guard asked for a physical description of Richard and his equipment. Richard wore a black wet suit and shouldered blue air tanks. The Coast Guard then radioed this information on a broadcast to all the ships in the area, just in case Richard had been swept away by the current and into the nearby shipping lane.

Dan then ordered the *Seeker's* inflatable Zodiac skiff into the water. Greg Mossfeldt and Bob Ryan took the small boat out. Keeping in touch with Dan with a handheld radio, Mossfeldt and Ryan took the Zodiac downwind of the *Seeker*, just in case Richard was drifting on the surface. They found nothing. As they bounced back to the *Seeker*, around 5 that afternoon, the Coast Guard radioed that it had dispatched a helicopter to the scene.

Dan asked John Moyer and Gary Gentile, both crew members on this trip and divers of almost unmatched experience on the *Andrea Doria*, to take the first search dives. Steve Berman, whose last dive had almost coincided with Richard's reported that when he left the shipwreck, the area around Gimbel's Hole was obscured in a cloud of silt. Could Richard have been in there? The group agreed that Moyer and Gentile should check. Dave Alderson recounted his conversation with Richard about the swimming pools. That was also good information. The search team would check the pools, too.

At 5:55, the Coast Guard helicopter from Cape Cod thundered in from the north and, its nose pointed slightly down, started sniffing across two search grids its crew had plotted around the *Seeker*. The Coast Guard pilot kept the HH-60 Jayhawk's altitude between seventy and one hundred feet. The helicopter crew radioed to Woods Hole that the visibility had dropped to less than a quarter mile. The crew dropped a buoy between the *Seeker* and *Wahoo* that would emit electronic signals and help the Coast Guard return to the spot.

At 6:30, as the helicopter raked its search field, Moyer and Gentile entered the water. Their specific information about the silting at Gimbel's Hole and the swimming pools was critical because their time as underwater searchers was so short. This was not like a search on land, where lines of people could walk shoulder-to-shoulder through the brush for hours. Moyer and Gentile had about twenty minutes once they got down to the wreck. Gentile checked Gimbel's Hole and swam forward to the ship's chapel and back to the kitchen positioned between the first-class and cabin-class dining rooms. Moyer swam along the Promenade Deck then veered down and toward the ship's stern to check the pools. About ten minutes after 7, Gentile scrawled a message on a diver's slate, tied it off to a inflated lift bag, clipped in to the *Seeker*'s anchor line, and sent it to the surface. "No sign of body in pool or Gimbel's Hole—no sign anywhere. Gary."

The sun slumped toward the horizon. As the sunset's colors drained from the sky, a gauze of fog began to unspool in ribbons around the wreck site. The water's surface took on a gunmetal color. The wind quickened to about fifteen miles per hour, and so the fog began to gather and shift in immense sheets that isolated the *Seeker* and the *Wahoo* from the rest of the Atlantic. The *Seeker* began to heave in the building swells.

Moyer and Gentile were doing their decompression stops when the Coast Guard helicopter turned back for Cape Cod.

The commanders had decided to send the helicopter back out at first light. Three more divers had entered the water just after Moyer and Gentile, but they had no success, either. As the sky darkened, the *Seeker* radioed the Coast Guard and asked it to notify Richard's family in Michigan about what had happened. He had been in the water for seven hours now. There was absolutely no doubt about his fate.

At 9 P.M., Dan gathered everyone aboard. The fog obscured the stars so the *Seeker* on the ocean was a small lamp lit in a huge, darkened room. They went over the areas to be searched the next day. Dan said they would "mow the lawn" and check every place a diver such as Richard could possibly have gone. The length of the Promenade Deck needed to be covered. The winding staircase leading from the Foyer Deck had to be checked. Someone needed to swim from the anchor chain forward to the bow. Divers were even assigned to comb the *Andrea Doria*'s debris field, where pieces of the liner's stack stuck out of the mud like monuments. The stack's red-and-green paint scheme—the colors of Italy—had long since been covered with several inches of scabby marine growth. The debris field probably was a long shot, because Richard had made plain his desire to go inside the ship and not waste precious time dropping to the bottom. Dan made sure every diver had a buddy for this search work. He told the divers that however they searched, he wanted no one else to place themselves at risk.

The Coast Guard made its telephone call to Clinton, Michigan, at 10:22 P.M. Richard Roost, Sr., a semi-retired tool and die maker, was home and sitting at his computer when the telephone rang. Roost and his son worked together in the dive shops, and the elder Roost could make custom fittings and tubes for his son's highly advanced scuba rigs. At first, Roost thought the call was a prank, and he prepared to hang up. He was not a well man; he had a paralyzed diaphragm, and he did not need any sort of aggravation. Then he realized that the call was legitimate. The knowledge stabbed his gut: He had lost the second of his three children in a span of a little more than a year.

He hung up the phone and trudged down the hall to the bedroom and woke up his wife, Roberta. Richard usually told his parents about his diving exploits after he returned. Otherwise, they worried too much. His mother openly opposed his going inside shipwrecks. But he had spoken to them about the *Andrea Doria* and had even shown them the deck plans. They knew he had gone to New York a few days earlier. They stayed up the whole night waiting for the phone to ring again and to talk more with the Coast Guard. They wanted to know that Richard had been found, that he was not lost forever in the ocean. But the Coast Guard did not place another call that night.

The Roosts called Scott Campbell, Richard's right-hand man at the dive shops, and he called Cyndee Roost at her apartment in Ypsilanti, a few miles east of Ann Arbor. Like the Roosts, she did not sleep that night either. Somehow she convinced herself that Richard had surfaced, alive, but that he was floating around unseen in the dark and growing cold.

At 5:15 the next morning, another helicopter lifted from the pavement at Air Station Cape Cod, which was located at sprawling Otis Air Force Base. Soon the helicopter was back over the two dive boats and resuming the search for Richard. But at 7:30, the Coast Guard had to pull the helicopter off the search so its crew could respond to another emergency. On the *Seeker,* Dan planned to make the first dive, and he and Greg Mossfeldt splashed into the water at 9:37 A.M. They checked areas around Gimbel's Hole—a dining room and a stairway. By 10:30, they were back to the *Seeker's* anchor line; Dan wrote "no find" on a slate and sent it up to the surface.

Ten more divers were in the water now swirling around the *Andrea Doria* like sharks circling a stricken whale, busily checking the mountainous wreck from every angle they could. All they found was a strobe light that Richard had clipped to the bottom of the *Seeker's* anchor line to help him get back to it at the end of his dive. The last divers in were John Moyer and Gary Gentile. The weather topside began to clear and the ambient light on the wreck began to subtly brighten. Jenn Samulski took a moment to record the weather: "CLEAR, SUNNY, W NW=5–10 KNTS. VIS UNLIMITED."

Once on the wreck, Moyer and Gentile headed to the Promenade Deck, the same place where Richard the previous morning had said it was impossible to get lost, where he had gazed from the interior darkness at the line of windows through which poured the comforting glow of the deep. The two divers swam well aft of the *Seeker's* anchor line and entered the wreck back by the cabin-class ballroom. It was about a quarter after 1 in the afternoon. Moyer swam high and Gentile swam low. At the midpoint of the ship, they passed through double doors that provided entry into the *Grande Bar Prima Classe,* the first-class lounge. Gentile knew this area well. In its heyday, this lounge had shimmered with mirrors and had a bar shaped like a horseshoe. Gentile had recovered a colorful set of enameled ceramic panels by Romano Rui here. Moyer checked his depth readout, which read 210 feet.

Then Gentile saw it.

Richard's body was wedged between two lounge tables, the bases of which, in the toppled-over orientation of the shipwreck, stuck out like turnstile arms from the left side, which had once been the floor of the lounge. Richard was at the bottom of this upturned room, exactly where a diver might be if he were looking for things that had fallen and could now be taken.

Gentile waved his light through the blackness to Moyer, and Moyer felt a wave of relief. Richard's arms were outstretched, pointed straight down in the push-up position. It looked as if he might have been combing the silt with his fingers for an artifact. He was neither entangled nor trapped. In his mouth he still appeared to clench his Poseidon regulator from his main air tanks. The way out was tantalizingly close: Windows were only fifty feet away. They were faintly lit from behind, and looked like a row of gelled theatrical lenses. This seemed to be the shadowy crevice of the wreck of the *Andrea Doria* where Richard had been for the previous twenty-four hours and twenty minutes.

Richard's gauges showed that his main tanks were empty. He had not attempted to use any of his decompression gases. Those tanks were full. Divers who suffered convulsions at depth spat out their regulators. Richard seemed as if he had simply fallen asleep. It was also puzzling to consider how Richard ended up in the first-class lounge. People normally did not stumble into this place; it was a sophisticated penetration. Maybe Richard had located the china closet two decks below and had become lost in the stairway that linked the two points.

Even Moyer and Gentile weren't certain exactly where they were, either in relation to the *Seeker's* anchor line or to the interior layout as they understood it. The interior morphed from season to season as the ship's passageways and decks folded in on each other. "Because of the collapse of the deck plating, we were uncertain of which deck we were on—promenade deck or boat deck," Gentile later wrote in his statement to the Coast Guard. The Boat Deck was above the Promenade Deck in the ship's correct orientation; now collapsed in places, they formed great odd-shaped caverns. Moyer and Gentile stuck their heads out the windows to get their bearings. Gentile then tied off one end of a line to a stanchion outside the wreck and the other end to Richard's left leg. Gentile pulled and Moyer pushed Richard's up and out of the wreck. Their planned bottom time was quickly running out, so they decided to let another team complete the recovery. They used Richard's own emergency ascent line to lash him the *Andrea Doria's* hull. Then Gentile sent up the slate: "Body Tied to Hull, 50 Ft FWD Our Line."

Dan and Greg Mossfeldt again dived together, at about 2:30. They found Richard on the hull, dragged his body over to the anchor line, and clipped him into the line. Mossfeldt then pressed the suit-inflation button on the chest of Richard's dry suit, which was hooked up to a gas bottle attached to Richard's leg. The suit filled with air and made Richard's body positively buoyant. It rose up the anchor line as on an elevator. When he popped to the surface, the weight of his tanks rolled him face-up, so his extended arms reached toward the sky.

Getting Richard's body aboard the *Seeker* took twenty minutes. The crew had to use the equipment davit to swing him on deck. The crew examined his equipment, but did not take it off Richard. Again, they saw that everything was in good working order. Half the stuff was brand new. Dan tested the air that was in Richard's buoyancy-control vest, which would be the same as the bottom Trimix he had breathed. The proportions of nitrogen, oxygen, and helium were exactly as Richard had indicated on Jenn's information sheets. Dan had checked in part to see if the oxygen was incorrectly elevated. If that had been the case, it might have suggested that Richard had succumbed to the toxic effects of oxygen under high pressure. But the mix was fine.

From that time forward, with no other evidence available to them, and even before the autopsy report was complete, Dan and the other divers involved became convinced that Richard had died due to a phenomenon known as "deep-water blackout." The phenomenon is little understood and rarely witnessed. Some divers have blacked out at great depths only to be revived when they are brought to shallower depths by their dive buddies. From Richard's empty tanks, the divers deduced that something had happened to Richard—something that rendered him unconscious—then he breathed all his air down and drowned. His body posture showed that he had not struggled and strongly suggested that he had no inkling of what had hit him at 210 feet inside the wreck. Their argument was persuasive but, of course, unproven.

This did not deter them from speculating about what killed Richard. This was part of their culture as deep divers; picking apart an accident helped them play out the multiple scenarios that they might be involved in some day. Deep-water blackout, with its mysterious triggers, also fit into the general view within the scuba diving community that held their sport was generally safe and that some people were just susceptible to unfathomed and deadly physical predispositions.

The *Seeker* got under way at about 4 on the afternoon of July 9. Richard's body remained locked in its beckoning pose in the boat's cockpit. Someone, out of respect or discomfort, covered it with a New York Mets beach towel.

At 9 the next morning, a jet from Detroit landed at Newark, New Jersey, carrying Cyndee Roost, Scott Campbell, and Richard's friend Neal Johnson. They rented a car and made it to Montauk by midafternoon. Richard's gear remained there, easily recognizable. Ever the Boy Scout, Richard had stenciled RJR or ROOST on every piece.

On the way back, now in the Divers, Inc., van that Richard had taken on his way out, the three had to stop in Hauppauge, Long Island, to identify Richard's body at the county medical examiner's. That night, somewhere along the road, they snapped open one of the plastic tubs that held Richard's belongings. He had used T-shirts as packing material. When they unrolled the shirts, there was the china Richard had retrieved from the *Doria*. Cyndee, Campbell, and Johnson all were divers, and they knew what kind of china they were holding: first class. Three saucers and one cup. Although the exposure to the air had robbed them of some of their luster, the pieces still glowed in the dashboard light.

Five days later, it looked as if disaster had struck outside the First United Methodist Church in Saline, Michigan. Every type of emergency vehicle—police cruisers, ambulances, fire engines—lined the road there. Law enforcement divers from the entire state had come to pay respects to the man they called Scuba God. Lee Somers, the University of Michigan professor who teamed with Richard to make presentations on diving safety, delivered remarks. His words reflected the unapologetic romanticism that characterizes many of today's deep divers, their view of themselves as urgently necessary interpreters of the mysteries of the deep or, at least, videographers of sunken tugboats and submarines and ocean liners, the last great explorers in the Age of the Couch Potato.

"Those who take risks can enjoy the exhilaration, the closeness to God, the serenity of the underwater world in ways that those who simply view television and live less adventurous lives cannot appreciate or understand," Somers said.

The funeral procession rolled for seventy miles along Highway 12 in southern Michigan and on to Frontier, Michigan, a small town on the Ohio border. Richard's father had grown up on a farm nearby, and Richard had asked to be buried there beside his grandparents.

The road to Frontier is two lanes of blacktop poured across rolling farm country, where weather-beaten barns appear to teeter on foundations of weathered stone. The procession motored through small towns joined by big curves in the pavement—Clinton, then Somerset, then Addison, then Hudson, where three midnight-blue grain silos bear the block-lettered legend, JESUS LOVES YOU.

In Frontier, trees canopied the cemetery, which was set between farms on a straight county road running south from Main Street. While pioneers' graves there bore heavily serifed dates and biblical send-offs, the newer markers showed off the latest in computerized etchings. One married couple was laid to rest under a stone depicting a camper and trailer, with GOING HOME written across the sky; another under a scene showing an old-fashioned plow leaning against a fence post.

Richard's marker more than met the requirement he laid out in the 1981 will. It was a thick panel of polished granite with a series of images. On the left appeared the international scuba diving symbol with its diagonal slash; on the right was etched the logo of Divers, Inc.; and in the center, Richard was illustrated in the chain-mail diving suit he wore while feeding the sharks in the Bahamas.

Richard's parents live in a brick, ranch-style house in Clinton that is set in a newer neighborhood subdivided from hilltop farmland. In their front yard, a waist-high chain-saw sculpture of Davy Crockett greets the neighbors. Richard had been obsessed with Davy Crockett in the 1950s—they bought him one of those coonskin caps, like so many parents—and his parents had found the sculpture at his son's home in Ann Arbor when they went to clean it out. Richard's father wore a shirt from the dive shop, where he was continuing to work part time.

"It keeps him close to Richard," Roberta Roost said.

"Well . . ." Richard Roost, Sr. said.

"It's true," Roberta said, quietly.

"I would say so," her husband agreed.

Their trauma was compounded by the mystery surrounding their son's death. Richard spoke about his son's reputation as a "shallow breather," which fit into one theory bandied about by the divers. They guessed that Richard had retained too much carbon dioxide in his system with his shallow breathing and might possibly have asphyxiated himself in this way.

The Roosts were proud of their son and delighted by him, too. As a high school student, he had been state champion in field archery at thirty, forty, and fifty yards. Those same steady hands made him a natural mechanic. They described him as "a thinker," but with a temper sometimes. They did not particularly like Cyndee Roost and thought the divorce a good idea. They didn't like the woman he was seeing at the time of his death, either. They talked at length about Richard's impish side. They displayed a photo of him drinking a bottle of soda underwater and another of him listening to music from a Walkman-like stereo while he hung on a decompression line. Then Roberta rose wordlessly from the table, went into the living room, and came back holding the three saucers and cup from the *Andrea Doria*.

"Here's what he took his life for," she said.

She said she hadn't yet decided whether to clean up the pieces. They still had stains from being underwater so long. She liked the idea that her son had left the china pieces in just this way. Still stained. He hadn't cleaned them up at all.

Then Roberta grew quiet for a moment.

She bit one side of her lip and cradled the cup. She moved it back and forth between her fingertips, sensing its weight.

Five

PARTIAL PRESSURES

On the day that Richard's friends identified his body at the county morgue on Long Island, Bill Cleary and Vince Napoliello spread out their deck plans of *Andrea Doria* and discussed the mistakes they had made on the wreck during their charter seven days earlier aboard the *Seeker*. Vince had become disoriented inside the seven-hundred-foot-long wreck. He smacked into a dead end where he'd thought a china closet was. Cleary noisily teased him about the screw-up, and Vince needled Cleary about dropping an expensive light on the same dive.

Neither of them knew Richard Roost, though Cleary knew Craig Sicola, who had died two weeks earlier. Word about Richard's death had just started to circulate. The delay was due in part to the belated announcement by the Coast Guard. It had not sent out a press release until 8:30 the night of the recovery. Reporters also could not easily talk to those aboard the *Seeker*. Divers from the charter scattered to their respective homes as soon as Dan pulled the boat into Star Island.

Cleary was hosting a party at his three-bedroom beach house in Brick, New Jersey, about ninety minutes south of New York. His guests were all divers. They included Vince Napoliello, his diving partner for the previous three years; Denis Murphy, a north Jersey police officer; and Bob Wilson, who was an instructor in technical diving. Vince and Murphy were scheduled to go with Cleary on a *Seeker* charter to the *Doria* in the first week of August. Cleary was there with his girlfriend, Vince with his fiancée, Marisa Gengaro, Murphy with his wife, Lisa, and Wilson with his wife, Karen.

Murphy asked a lot of questions about exploring the ship. He was not easily cowed, having worked as a cop for several years and having trained attack dogs in the Army. But he had enough diving experience to expect the unexpected at scuba diving's premier wreck dive.

People were drinking, and the party got loud that night, and the neighbors complained. While the men pored over the deck plans in the dining room, the women gathered in the kitchen. One of the women was a jeweler, and she and Marisa talked about rings. She and Vince were to be married the following spring. She couldn't help overhearing the men's conversation, and she enjoyed lobbing a few bombs their way.

"You guys are crazy!" she yelled. "Are you really ready for this? Jesus, it's dangerous."

Vince threw back a remark about Marisa's smoking. She was as thin as a runway model, and she smoked a lot, especially when she was nervous. He wanted her to quit.

"Be careful," she replied. "Vince, *be careful.*"

Richard's death soon seemed to be drawing more attention than Craig Sicola's. The drawn-out search effort eventually had given the Coast Guard district headquarters in Boston time to pump out two press releases. The public relations staff even got permission to attribute a quotation to Rear Admiral Richard M. Larrabee, the commander of the Coast Guard's First District. "This incident is another tragic example of the dangers associated with recreational deep water diving," the admiral was quot-

Andrea Doria, *pride of the Italian fleet.*

The crippled
Stockholm *after the collision.*

The Andrea Doria *as she listed to starboard.*

The Andrea Doria *sinking by the bow in this spectacular aerial shot by Harry Trask. The airplane's wing is visible at the bottom of the image. The pilot ducked so that Trask could take the photos in this sequence.*

The lifeboats
and deck debris were
crushed as the Doria
rolled and sank.

Above, the final image of the Andrea Doria *before she sank.*

*Below, after fifty years underwater, the "A"
on the* Andrea Doria's *stern is still visible.*

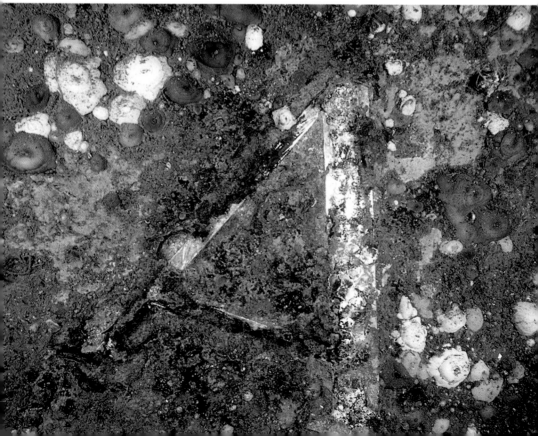

A huge mound of second-class china plates found lying inside a stairwell.

Daniel Crowell, captain of the Seeker, *talks about the death of Charles McGurr while docked at Star Island.*

Dan Crowell and the Seeker.

Diver completing
a lengthy decompression
after a productive dive to the Doria.

Above, Craig Sicola relaxing on the Seeker.

Below, a glass-topped table inside the Doria's *first-class cocktail lounge.*

Marisa Gengaro pauses at the closet in her New Jersey apartment that still holds the clothes of her fiancée, Vincent Napoliello.

MICHAEL E. ACH © NEWSDAY

Vince Napoliello on a 1996 trip with china from the Andrea Doria.

Above, Richard Roost after a dive from the Seeker.

Below, Richard Roost, Jr.'s grave in Frontier, Michigan.

Roberta and Richard Roost, Sr., examining the first-class china their son collected from the wreck of the Andrea Doria *on the day before he died.*

Chris Murley at Gilboa Quarry near Cincinnati,
where he conducted dive training.

Chris Murley at Montauk, NY on July 19, 1999, shortly before his death.

Chris Murley on a dive in Italy.

Nick Caruso with sons Christopher and Joseph.

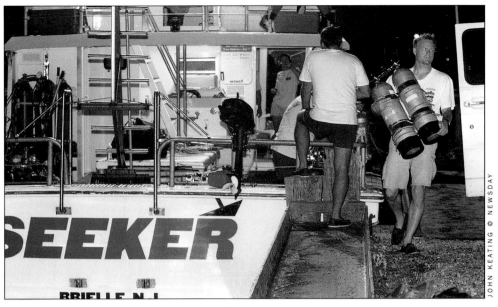

Joe King (right), takes his diving tanks off the Seeker *after returning from the trip where Charlie McGurr died.*

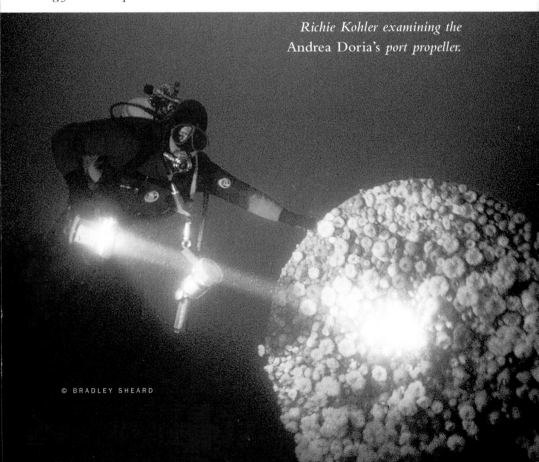

Richie Kohler examining the Andrea Doria's *port propeller.*

A diver at the Andrea Doria's stern during conditions of exceptional visibility.

ed as saying. "The Coast Guard strongly encourages all people who are involved in this activity to take appropriate precautions before diving on deep water wrecks. We recommend that you research the dive site, taking into account weather and currents. We also recommend that you check with a nationally recognized diving organization before chartering a dive boat."

While Dan appreciated the Coast Guard helicopter crews who had responded to his boat's emergencies, he was simultaneously amused and maddened by headquarters statements such as Larrabee's. The Coast Guard treated the exploration of deep-sea destinations such as the *Andrea Doria* as if the wreck were a guided tour for which every contingency could be anticipated. He knew Bob Higgins, a senior marine-safety investigator with the First District, had extensive dive experience, but Higgins never led the probes of any *Andrea Doria* fatalities. Lieutenant Tim Dickerson did, and what did he know? As far as Dan was concerned, the agency was clueless.

Of course *Andrea Doria* divers researched their dive sites—not only was it essential for safety, but it was half the fun for many of the divers, who were maritime history buffs. People needed to understand that sometimes, things just happened. Shit happened, Dan liked to say, even to the best.

Nevertheless, at times the Coast Guard seemed to be articulating a case for regulating offshore scuba diving. *The Detroit News* published a story about Richard that quoted a Coast Guard official as saying, "A lot of people visit the area, and we really can't keep track of how many people are out there at any particular time." The Associated Press sent a reporter to Cape Cod who interviewed a Hyannis dive shop owner. "I've got 2,500 recreational dives and I still have never done the *Doria*," said the owner, Mike Walls. "I'd have to take classes from other divers."

These kinds of statements drew a shoulder shrug and a smirk from Dan. For all their self-identification as the last of America's true adventurers (the ocean was the last remaining unexplored place), the top divers did not think, as they rode the *Seeker* to the wreck, "Ooooo, we are about to challenge the Mount Everest of scuba diving." Other top divers confirmed this, but for them it may be that the novelty of the site had worn away. To the extent the wreck could be mastered, they had done so. But many other divers did consider the *Andrea Doria* the pinnacle of their underwater careers. Craig Sicola and Richard Roost, who were more typical of the sport than Dan Crowell and his friends, told people they felt this way. Dan's larger point, however, was that the tragedies that had taken place at the *Andrea Doria* were not the result of a mythic shipwreck having overwhelmed the divers. One man disobeyed his training, and the other apparently had a physical problem strike him out of the blue. These dives could be made with reasonable safety, but not total safety.

As John Chatterton said, "Society as a whole likes to think we're going to make this thing safe. Some things just have an inherent danger in them. Mountain climbing is one of those things. This kind of wreck diving is another."

The media coverage served to keep Craig Sicola and Richard Roost at the front of Dan's mind. Of course, he said, he would not forget either man, but at the same time, Dan wanted to look forward. He had most of the summer stretching before him with his popular boat booked every weekend. He considered himself optimistic.

Both articles also mentioned the death of Craig Sicola, and the Associated Press account listed some of the other diving deaths that had occurred off the deck of the *Seeker*. Coast Guard and police records also showed that, counting Craig Sicola and Richard Roost, five *Seeker* divers had now perished at the wreck of the *Andrea Doria*. The last death of a *Seeker* diver at the wreck had occurred in 1992, before Dan had taken over the boat's operation.

Michael William Scofield, thirty-six, a diver from Soquel, California, had apparently become lost inside the ship, run low on air, passed out and drowned. That same summer—thirteen days earlier—Matthew G. Lawrence, thirty-two, of Miami Lakes, Florida, had drowned fourteen minutes into his dive, his death apparently triggered by poorly mixed breathing gases that contained an inadequate amount of oxygen. In 1988, Joe Drozd, forty-two, of Stonington, Connecticut, had become entangled in free-drifting fishing line that had locked up around his air tanks, cut himself free, became disoriented, spat out his regulator, and drowned.

Since 1981, nine divers overall had died at the *Andrea Doria*. One dived from the *Sea Hunter I* charter boat, one from *Sea Hunter III*, two from the *Wahoo,* and five from the *Seeker*. Craig Sicola's death represented the first fatality from the *Seeker* at the *Andrea Doria* since Scofield had perished six years earlier. Dan felt that, more than just about anything, the odds had simply overtaken the boat.

Additional divers had died using the *Seeker* as a platform to explore other wrecks. The top echelon of divers also knew that Dan and Chatterton had skippered the *Seeker* in October 1992 when Chris and Chrissy Rouse, a father–son team, had died exploring a World War II–era submarine in the Atlantic Ocean halfway between the New York and New Jersey shorelines. So just as Dan had expected, talk percolated once again about the "the death boat." It bothered him. He knew that people with real insight on diving the *Andrea Doria* would not blame him, or the *Seeker*'s crew, for what had happened that summer, but he could not account for the majority—those outside the inner circle. At a minimum, the publicity was not good for business.

As a joke, a diver on Dan's next charter ceremoniously produced his own body bag. Just in case, the diver indicated.

Dan didn't laugh much.

Two weeks after Richard's death, Dan had the *Seeker* moored again into the wreck of the *Doria*. The charter aboard had been organized by Joe Jackson, a manager and instructor at the Cincinnati Diving Center. Jackson booked a few charters each summer aboard the *Seeker*, so he and Dan were well acquainted. Jackson was an ex-cop and a fourteen-year Marine Corps veteran; he had trained divers for the Corps and for the U.S. Navy. Over time, Dan came to trust Jackson to sign up only competent divers. If Jackson vouched for a diver's quality, that was good enough for Dan.

Among the divers aboard was a man named Jack Moulliett. He was a forty-seven-year-old chemical salesman who had done more than fifty dives on the *Andrea Doria*, which was an extraordinary number. He was not Dan Crowell's favorite diver, however, because Dan thought Moulliett was too cheap with the gear he bought and nursed along for years.

Alone, Moulliett was diving on air (cheaper than using the

Trimix breathing gases) and enjoying a productive dive on the wreck when a cascade of bad things happened to him. He was using a safety line that day—albeit an eighth-inch line, a cheap nylon model—so he could leave the china hole he was plundering with no guessing as to the way out.

He had several dishes already in his bag when one slipped from his hand and fell. As Moulliett watched, the plate pitched back and forth like a leaf in a breeze and somehow landed squarely and undamaged on a steel ledge about ten feet deeper into the wreck.

Moulliet decided to drop down and retrieve the plate. He did so and was settling the booty into his mesh bag when he spotted another dish on the ledge. He pivoted his body to reach that plate, grabbed it, and nestled it into the bag. As he began to creep upward, he felt his body being tugged to the side. His lightweight nylon safety line had become entwined in the air tank valves behind his head.

With his bottom gases running out, Moulliett realized his was a textbook scenario for accidental diving death. He tried to pirouette out of the snare, but that made it worse. He had made a web out of his safety line and now he was caught in it. As he struggled, he found that he was dropping deeper into the wreck. He was at 225 feet, and the phenomenon of oxygen toxicity now became a real concern. So he grabbed one of his dive knives, flat in a sleeve on his leg, and was about to cut it when he grew fearful that the freed line would then fall back on him and tighten the web. He replaced his knife and took the time to painstakingly free himself from the coils. All this had taken five minutes—five minutes he did not have. He was almost out of air.

Then, as he ascended inside the ship and made his way out, Moulliett couldn't properly draw air from his regulator. He wondered whether the safety line had gripped the knob on his isolator valve, which was located on a manifold between his two main air tanks and which allowed air to flow into the regulator hose from both those tanks. The configuration essentially made a single air source out of the two main tanks. Sometimes, the knob could get hung up in lines, and it led divers to believe that their air was cut off when actually their valve had simply rotated by accident and shut down one tank. But Moulliett's isolator valve seemed OK.

Now he felt starved for a breath of air. He decided he would make a dash for his sixty-foot decompression stop. There, he could breathe safely on his oxygen-rich decompression gas tanks.

He made the sprint, climbing over a couple of divers hanging there and never asking for assistance. But when he tried to breathe on his decompression tank, he heard a bang, like a hammer striking steel, and a rush of bubbles exploded to the surface. The O-ring seal at the top of the tank had blown. He decided to ascend as fast as he could.

He climbed the *Seeker*'s anchor line, stepping over more divers who could have helped him. Holding his breath, he felt the rising pressure expand his lungs and tickle the back of his throat.

"Help!" he screamed as he heaved to the surface. "I need air!"

Dan was on deck and sprang into action even as his anger began to boil. It was obvious that Moulliett had not even thought to use one of the regulators dangling in the water twenty feet below, which were hooked up to oxygen tanks on the boat. He had also climbed over other divers who could have helped. Dan climbed to the wheelhouse and punched up some decompression software to calculate how long he would keep Moulliett underwater to keep him from getting the bends.

Normally a diver would take about an hour to ascend methodically from two hundred feet. Moulliett would need much more time than that to compensate for his dangerously fast sprint to the surface. Dan instructed two other divers to take a fresh set of tanks for Moulliett. He would need to stay down in the cold water for four more hours before his body had properly decompressed and he could come back aboard.

The emergency resolved, Dan felt a wave of fatigue buffet his body. He had to sit down. He needed to be quiet. His thoughts drifted to his last two emergencies. Craig and Richard. It had been less than a month. Two men dead. A third man probably should be dead, given what had happened. Events were undermining the dependable mortar that neatly kept Dan's emotions in check, and he suddenly could feel the tremors. He found a corner of the boat and began to cry.

"What the hell are these guys doing?" he recalled thinking. "This guy was No. 3, and we pulled him through it, and then it becomes apparent that he did something extremely stupid."

Joe Jackson said that Dan cried for half an hour that afternoon.

When Jack Moulliett finally limped up the ladder, shivering and hungry, Dan let him have it. He called him a cheap, panicking asshole who almost got himself killed. He didn't let up. Moulliett wanted to fire back at Dan, but he appreciated what Dan had done for him too much to do that. He did feel like an idiot. He had made mistakes. This had been his first dive of the year; normally, divers make several preparatory dives per season before dropping down to the *Andrea Doria*. He wished he hadn't acknowledged that his malfunctioning regulator was at least ten years old. Dan had fun with that one. Cheap bastard! Still, Dan's incessant verbal abuse did trigger Moulliett to say to himself, "Dan, you lost two divers. If those divers would have kept their heads like I did, maybe they'd be alive."

"Dan and I don't mesh real good," Moulliett said. "Our personalities clash. Dan comes across as the perfect diver. He's never had a problem. Whereas I know for a fact that I know people who have dived with Dan, and I know he has had problems. But it's bad to disagree with Dan. He's used to a lot of yes-people."

Dan had no more use for Jack Moulliett. He understood that bad things happened sometimes, but Moulliett had been careless in the preparation of his gear and had panicked like a first-time pool diver with his absurd ascent. Worst of all, Moulliett had made his desperate race for the surface without unclipping his goodie bag bulging with china. Moulliett, thought Dan, was careless and greedy.

It was all unforgivable. Leading ten charters per season to the *Andrea Doria*, Dan couldn't afford to have such sloppy diving taking place off his decks. From that day forward, Dan said, Jack Moulliett was never to dive again off the *Seeker*.

To describe Moulliett's status, Dan tossed off a phrase a boy might use to restrict access to a secret tree house. Jack Moulliett, Dan declared, was "banished for life."

Six

On February 13, 1998, Marisa Gengaro, who taught at a private school in Manhattan, came home to her high-rise apartment in Jersey City and found an elaborate invitation piled at her doorway. A teddy bear dressed in a tuxedo sat amid a dozen red roses and a note: "Wear your best clothes. A car will pick you up at 6:30." It was from Vince Napoliello. That night, at a Manhattan restaurant, Vince proposed, and Marisa accepted. Soon they picked out a date—April 24 of the following year. A Saturday wedding in Roseland at the Blessed Sacrament Roman Catholic Church would be followed by a reception at the Montclair Golf Club. They even picked the first song they would dance to: "In Your Eyes," the quirky pop ballad by Peter Gabriel.

Vince's engagement seemed, to his friends, to reflect his growing maturity. He was hitting his stride as a financial adviser at Legg Mason, an investment banking firm with offices in Lower Manhattan. His best friend at the firm, David Murphy, saw Vince working harder and smarter. Vince had begun to tap into a lucrative network of physicians, in part because his father was a surgeon in Pompton Plains, a leafy suburb in northern New Jersey. Vince had made a six-figure income the previous two years. As much as anything, his natural charm and good humor propelled him. Six feet tall and 180 pounds, he had a brilliant smile, floppy black hair, and stylishly long sideburns. He wore suits from Brooks Brothers, which was the uniform for the conservative firm where he worked, but he accessorized them with chunky cuff links shaped like anchors. The women who worked in the Legg Mason suite couldn't help noticing Vince, and he enjoyed the flirting that went on. He put on goofy costumes at broker-association dances, led a Wall Street dart team and, attuned to the late-1990s trend, he liked to hand out Cuban cigars. "If you put him in a room," David Murphy said, "by the end of the night, he knew most of the people in that room, and that is a very important skill in this business."

Vince's obsession with diving and the ocean was plain to anyone who entered his office at Legg Mason. He had hung a framed poster depicting the bottom of the ocean there. It was the same at his apartment in Brooklyn Heights, where he had mounted deck plans of the *Andrea Doria* on the wall above a display case containing artifacts he had brought from the wreck. He also had a lobster claw as big as his arm up on the wall; he loved telling people about finding that monster down on the bottom on one of his dives.

Vince's passion for wreck diving had begun to wane, however. The reason was simple. He had seen most of the major Northeast wrecks. He still wanted to refine his skill in technical diving—he was gaining his Trimix certification only that spring—but he decided he would focus his future dives on the most compelling wrecks. He was fascinated by the *U-869*, the German World War II submarine that John Chatterton had identified and had been detailed in a Discovery Channel film. But he wasn't thrilled about returning to some of the more well-surveyed "mud hole" wrecks in the dark waters between New York and New Jersey. He failed to see the payoff in slogging through the bottom ooze to explore a sunken freighter.

He and Chatterton met at a Hoboken restaurant for dinner early that summer, and he told Chatterton as much. At a boat show around the same time, he told David Murphy that had also had more personal reasons for cutting back on expeditions to sites such as the *Andrea Doria*. He wanted his marriage to succeed, and was excited about his accelerating Wall Street career. He had started to feel he was being selfish with all the diving, weekend after weekend. He said it didn't seem fair to Marisa. Vince was certain this would be his last dive on the *Andrea Doria*.

Vince woke up on August 3 and gathered a few of his things for the midweek dive charter to the *Doria*. Marisa had baked Toll House chocolate chip cookies for each of his three previous trips to the wreck, but not this time. Vince liked everything just so. He had taken delicious home-baked treats on the other *Andrea Doria* trips, so why not this time? But it was Monday morning and Marisa told him she had too many things to think about at the beginning of the week and now her boyfriend was whining about cookies.

"You didn't make the cookies," Vince said.

"No, I told you, I didn't have time," she replied.

"Well," he said, and he turned on the big white smile, "if I don't come back, you'll know that's the reason."

Marisa, who wished Vince did not feel the urge to dive the *Andrea Doria* anymore, erupted. "Vincent, don't say that. Don't pressure me. I don't need the pressure. I'm trying to go to work. That's not fair. Don't say that."

He apologized and went across the Hudson River and over to Whitehall Street, where the Legg Mason offices took up the twenty-sixth floor at One Battery Park Plaza. He was training a new assistant that day and did not get to Montauk until past 8. Bill Cleary, who had hosted the barbecue at his beach house a few weeks earlier, was there, as was Denis Murphy, the broad-shouldered police officer making his first dive on the *Doria*. After dinner at Gurney's Inn that night, they smoked cigars and couldn't help breaking into passages of twisted dialogue from *Scarface,* their favorite Al Pacino film. "First you get the money," Cleary said, "then you get the power." Now the others joined in: "*Then you get the woman.*"

Cleary basked in the company of these particular divers; he and Murphy had met at Blue Water Divers, a scuba shop on Highway 17 not far from Cleary's law office, and he and Vince had been teaming up for three seasons. Fiery, with an emotional fragility at odds with his bodybuilder physique, Cleary looked up to Vince, who projected solidity with enviable nonchalance. Cleary's enthusiasm for technical diving was rooted in schmaltzy romanticism; at his barbecue the week before, he felt deeply as if he and the other divers were going off to war. At Gurney's that night, no one drank much at all, because it's not considered safe to drink and dive, but most brought alcohol for the ride back, after the dives. While others packed six-packs of beer for themselves, Vince brought a bottle of twenty-year-old Scotch for everyone to enjoy.

Back at the Star Island docks, as Dan idled the *Seeker's* engines, Vince told everyone to huddle up around one of his equipment boxes. He flipped the lid open. Inside were three bags of potatoes, a tube fused from lengths of plastic pipe, and a can of hair spray. It was a crude mortar, what the men called a "potato cannon." Vince had heard that the *Sea Inn*, another New Jersey diving charter boat, also planned to be anchored into the *Andrea Doria* for the next few days. Nick Caruso, the usual dive-team leader on the *Sea Inn*, and Dan Crowell were not on good terms. Everyone knew that, and Vince proposed to attack the *Sea Inn* with the potato cannon. The other *Seeker* men, giggling like high school pranksters, agreed that Vince's idea was an excellent one.

Dan cast off the *Seeker*'s lines about 10:30 P.M. and turned the boat toward Montauk Inlet. The night was still warm, with temperatures in the sixties, and the *Seeker* splashed through the black water under the bright beacon of a waxing moon. Vince grabbed his cell phone and headed for the bow. He had a hand-me-down phone from his father, one of the old, bag-style cells, and he found he could get a stronger signal from the bow. He planned to use the phone to check in with work during the week, though now he dialed Marisa's number in Jersey City.

"We're just hanging out, driving out to the wreck," Vince told her. "It's a beautiful night."

Then he launched into one of his safety routines. He could be neurotic about safety. In a precaution all but unheard of among Northeast scuba divers, he attached an EPIRB to his dry suit. The EPIRB, which bounced a radio signal off satellites to guide rescuers, was the sort of sophisticated device found on commercial fishing boats that sailed offshore. He was a cautious man on dry land as well, prepared for any contingency. Marisa found this quality mildly irritating but lovable. When she'd gotten her Ford Explorer, he'd loaded up the back end with shovels, flares, and tubes of flat-fixing goop. Once, when they were driving together, she started applying her eyeliner, and he pulled over and announced he wouldn't go on until she was "done with those sticks." He pronounced her makeup application dangerous. Marisa usually fired back at him that *he* was the one crawling around blind inside shipwrecks in two hundred feet of water. *That* was dangerous, she said. Now, on the phone from the *Seeker*, he urged her not to take the PATH commuter train at night, and to be careful around the station in Jersey City.

"Be careful walking the dog at night, OK?" he said.

"Vince, *you* be careful."

"I love you. The phone's breaking up here. I'll see you Thursday."

When the *Seeker* divers awoke the next morning, they saw that the *Sea Inn* was already moored on the wreck of the *Andrea Doria*—about fifty yards away, well within the agreed-upon range of the potato cannon. The *Sea Inn* was a handsome boat. Its hull was fire-engine red, with the boat's named spelled in gold letters on the transom; a low-slung wheelhouse sat far forward with a long canopy shading the deck. The Northeast technical-diving fraternity is small, and a few of the *Sea Inn* divers had previously dived off the *Seeker*. They included Steve Gatto, the south Jersey electrician who had been aboard the *Seeker* for Craig Sicola's fatal dive; Santiago Garcia, who owned a hardware store in the Bronx; Tommy Surowiec, a police officer, in Union City, New Jersey, and his wife, Joanne, also an experienced diver; and Nick Caruso.

Caruso was part owner of Sea Dwellers, a dive shop in Hillsdale. Garcia and Surowiec didn't associate themselves with the *Seeker* much anymore, and Caruso was, like Jack Moulliett, banished for life (he and Dan had had a disagreement over money). Garcia said he always felt a distance between charter customers such as him and Dan and his pals. Surowiec got sick of listening to Dan and the others trash whoever was not in earshot and also to the bickering between Dan and Jenn Samulski. Both men, however, thought Dan the consummate professional captain and a gifted diver. Surowiec also believed that Dan ran a safe boat, but Caruso disagreed.

He thought egos overshadowed safety on the *Seeker*. He couldn't understand why relative novices on the *Andrea Doria* such as Craig Sicola and Richard Roost had been allowed to penetrate the ship so aggressively. He thought the accidents were preventable. He told people that Dan shared blame for those deaths.

But in Northeast diving, opinions always had a back story, and facts often were distorted by rival agendas. Many divers, those who were loyal crew members of Dan's and those such as Tommy Surowiec, who had a more independent perspective, believed Caruso operated with a bias that darkened his view toward Dan and led him to denigrate a competitor. Six summers before, when Bill Nagle still ran the *Seeker*, Caruso had dived off the boat with Matthew Lawrence at the *Andrea Doria*, and Lawrence had been killed at the wreck. They had split up while exploring the ship, and Caruso had become tangled in a penetration line while inside the wreck. When he came out, he had almost run out of air.

He swam to where the two men had left their decompression air canisters (without tying them off, as other divers loved to point out with disgust in their voices), grabbed his tanks and saw that Lawrence had not yet returned. Because both men had descended together, Lawrence's absence was a tip-off. He probably was in trouble. But Caruso, with virtually no air and therefore no time, proceeded with his decompression and eventually ascended. Lawrence's dead body was later found at a depth of 254 feet—he had apparently fallen to this alarming depth after he became incapacitated—and his gauges showed he'd run out of air. Many held the view that Caruso and Lawrence didn't know what they were doing. Lawrence's death was especially senseless in a sport where people had a high tolerance for senselessness, where divers courted extreme danger to recover gift shop gewgaws.

In retrospect, what Caruso had done did not seem different in character than what technical divers frequently do: They look out for themselves. Their training teaches them to be self-reliant. If the sport is governed by anything, it's the general expectation that the various certifications really should be meaningful and that everyone can take care of himself. Craig Sicola had been allowed to dive alone, as had Richard Roost. Caruso remains genuinely disturbed about Lawrence's death; they had dived as partners for three seasons. He kept a photograph of Lawrence in his living room for years. And yet, something about Caruso's style rubbed people the wrong way. He seemed drawn to confrontation, and he couldn't come close to Dan Crowell's unstudied coolness and edgy wit. He kept saying he was about to debut his own dive boat, but never did. People even ridiculed Caruso's business card, which showed him piloting an underwater scooter emblazoned with the profile of a toothy, snarling shark. Chatterton recalled Billy Deans, the technical-diving pioneer, being so ruffled by Caruso's diving that he offered Caruso free Trimix lessons on the spot, and that Caruso had fired back a dismissive response. Chatterton was shocked that someone would show what he viewed as disrespect toward Deans, who qualified as a historic figure in modern scuba diving. Nick Caruso found himself continually ground up in the backbiting world of Northeast technical diving, but he seemed to do himself few favors.

August 4 dawned as a spectacular day to dive. The temperature reached seventy degrees in the morning. The heat cooked the divers, who were sheathed in neoprene suits, but a ten-mile-an-hour breeze from the southeast took the edge off. Visibility stretched twenty miles, almost halfway to Nantucket Island. The lazy current moved at less than half a knot per hour. Divers could move easily from the *Seeker* to the anchor line that plunged into the darkness. Visibility promised to be better than average at the wreck's depth, and Dan Crowell decided to take his camera below and get more shots for the video he wanted to make of the wreck.

Bill Cleary, Denis Murphy, and Vince Napoliello dived as a team. Cleary and Murphy stepped off the diamond-plate panel along the *Seeker*'s rail at 9 A.M., and Vince followed four minutes later. They planned to use the permanent guide line attached inside Gimbel's Hole to penetrate the ship. They had talked about how they would proceed at Cleary's barbecue the previous weekend. When Vince caught up with them down where the anchor line was hooked in to the shipwreck, they all gathered together, like sky divers meeting heads-first with their feet straight back behind them. They remained silent for a few beats, then broke out laughing inside their masks. Water is an excellent conductor of sound, and they could hear each other breaking up. They made each other laugh with mock-serious expressions that said, "The men have begun their adventure!" They were giddy. They were diving the *Andrea Doria*.

Murphy, the first-timer, joined in the laughter, but he also felt overwhelmed by the darkness at 180 feet. The sheer size of the wreck was also a shocker. He had studied the ship's drawings and he knew that beyond the darkness—beyond the forty feet of visibility in the blue-green water—the ruin of the *Andrea Doria* continued for another several hundred feet, that he was standing next to an almost hundred-story building on its side. He was in awe. He understood what so many divers had told him, that when their fins hit the wreck's portside hull, they thought that they had touched bottom: It took five minutes to get there, even with weights on, and the hull was pulsing with marine growth, with snails as big as baseballs. The ship was monumental in all directions. Murphy could not picture what the stern or the bow must look like.

The three divers pumped their fins gently and swam down to Gimbel's Hole. Their diving lights fell upon the penetration line there. They dropped briefly into the wide chute and were ascending back out of the ship when Cleary got tangled in the line, which snaked around the knob on his isolator valve. Most divers keep the knob in the open position. That way, they can draw down the air from both tanks. If a diver closes the knob and does not realize this, it would feel as if he or she were out of air, when in fact only one of the tanks had been emptied. Many divers keep the valve open in a way that seems potentially dangerous to the novice. They close the knob tight all the way, then crack it back open so the valve is open just enough to allow the transfer of gas through the manifold. By leaving the valve open only as much as precisely required, a diver can close it quickly with a quarter turn of the knob or so—in case he or she needs to cut a supply of bad air in an emergency. But the diver has to remember to open it back up. Otherwise, he might create his own emergency.

Cleary's predicament could have been serious if he had been alone. Under the circumstances, he was free in about thirty seconds. Vince carefully unlooped the penetration line from Cleary's tanks, and the three men then swam to the *Seeker's* anchor line and began their decompression schedules. They surfaced by about 10:30 that morning.

They all planned to wait about four hours before going back in the water. They spent some of that time resting, adjusting their gear, and helping the other divers lift themselves back on deck. Vince decided to take advantage of the large oxygen bottle Dan kept on the *Seeker*. The oxygen allowed the divers to mix their own breathing gases. It was another amenity that marked the *Seeker* as a special charter boat. Its divers felt confident enough to mix their own gas, while most others were content to lug along canisters that they had ordered premixed at dive shops back home.

Vince apparently added oxygen to his 80 percent decompression cylinder, which he had partially drained during his last few decompression stops—those that were closest to the surface. He had sucked some down some of that tank, but by now topping it off with pure oxygen, he had created a 36 percent oxygen tank (it contained 36 percent oxygen and 64 percent nitrogen). He could use the 36 percent mix at his deepest decompression stops, the ones closer to the wreck.

The tank still had a piece of tape on it that labeled it as 81.3 percent oxygen, but Vince knew it was 36 percent. It was odd that Vince, the safety obsessive, did not change his tank labels. As a rule, technical divers are careful about the labels; if they breathe from a high-oxygen tank at, say, below one hundred feet, the oxygen can be toxic and cause them to convulse and spit out their regulator. The condition known as oxygen toxicity is a regular contributor to deep-diving deaths. So divers usually make an effort to label their tanks distinctly. As a backup, many adopt personal color codes to mate their different tanks with their associated regulators. Vince used a green regulator for his shallow-decompression regulator, which was hooked up to the tank with the higher oxygen content, and a yellow regulator for his deep-decompression regulator, hooked to the tank with a lower fraction of oxygen.

Vince slipped into his white-soled boat shoes, and he heard the usual "Yuppie!" jeers from his diving friends, including Murphy. "Bald bastard," Vince growled in mock consternation to Murphy, who had shaved his head. They really unloaded on him when he put on the beaten-up pair of flannel pants he usually brought along, for times when the temperatures cooled in the evening. He grabbed the big cell phone and headed for the bow.

He made several calls to Legg Mason. He and David Murphy commiserated about the market, which was headed for a three-hundred-point drop that day. It was the third largest point drop ever for the Dow. Vince steered his clients to aggressive-growth issues, and the sell-off on Wall Street hurt. As the afternoon wore on, Vince returned to the bow a few times to make more calls. He didn't take time to rest. He talked and talked. He realized he had to address a margin call before the market closed at 4 P.M. The sagging Dow had left one of his clients' portion of a stock purchase short of cash. He had to track that person down by the end of trading. It wasn't a good day to have a new assistant back at the office, and it wasn't a good day to be a hundred miles away. Vince got the margin call nailed down, but it was almost 3 in the afternoon.

He and Murphy had decided they would go back in the water at about 3:30. He was so distracted he didn't tell Jenn Samulski how long he planned to spend on the wreck during his second dive or the dive's anticipated total run time. She or another crew member recorded such information for every diver, every trip. That way, she knew when someone was over-due. Vince was the only diver to fail to supply such information that afternoon. Cleary thought Vince looked agitated. He encouraged his friend to relax.

While Cleary stated his intention to swim outside the ship on his afternoon dive, around the Winter Garden walkway that had once wrapped around the forward portion of the *Andrea Doria*'s Promenade Deck, Vince and Murphy agreed they wanted to get inside—to the china closet. It would be a significant penetration for Murphy, the rookie on the wreck. Vince assured him he could handle it. Murphy loved the idea of bringing back some china. He couldn't resist it. It's how the divers kept score, and he wanted to be on the scoreboard. Vince told Murphy about how he and Cleary had worked as a team the previous month and had come back with twenty pieces of china. One would hold the light and the other would remove pieces from the china closet.

This season, to dislodge china embedded in the silt, and to bring it within an arm's reach, the divers were all using a long-handled, stainless-steel rake that one of the divers had fashioned. Successive divers used the rake, then left it for the next diver. Murphy said it sounded perfect.

They went over to the knee-high steel table near the *Seeker*'s stern where the divers sat to make it easier to get into their scuba gear. Two divers helping out there noticed the labels on Vince's decompression tanks. Under the typical gear arrangement favored by most technical divers who use Trimix, both of Vince's decompression tanks hung in front of him, almost tucked under each of his arms. Mike Wagner noticed that one tank was was labeled "83%," but that the other read "81.3%."

Why was Vince packing two tanks filled with a mix appropriate only for the shallow-decompression stops? One of them should have been filled with a mix containing a lower proportion of oxygen. Two 80 percent cans didn't make sense.

Vince explained that the right-side tank actually contained only 36 percent oxygen, which was OK for the deeper decompression stops. Dean Repola was assisting also, and he asked Vince the same question. Again, Vince assured him that his right-side decompression tank contained the 36 percent mix. He had blended it himself earlier that afternoon.

"Are you sure?" Repola asked.

"Yes," said Vince.

"You're sure?"

"I'm sure."

Vince and Murphy jumped in the water at 3:40 P.M. Vince got to the anchor line first, and they decended the line almost as one unit, with Murphy close behind. Murphy was so close he rested his forearm on top of Vince's main tanks. They descended quickly. It was if the ship were sucking them down. When they hit the hull of the liner, they saw their friend Cleary approaching. He had hit the water fourteen minutes earlier and was just now wrapping up his tour of the Winter Garden. Once again they all gathered in heads-first fashion; Vince took Cleary's arm with one hand and, with the other, touched his thumb and index finger in the OK sign. He meant it as question. Had his dive gone well? Cleary nodded his head in assent. But Vince would not let go of Cleary's arm until Cleary, laughing, had made the OK sign in response. The official technical-diver underwater signaling *must* be used! Then Cleary inched up the anchor line to his first decompression stop.

Vince and Murphy dipped their heads and began kicking toward Gimbel's Hole. At about this time, Dan Crowell and John Moyer were stepping off the *Seeker*, with Dan cradling his underwater video camera. Vince and Murphy dropped feetfirst into Gimbel's. They descended roughly thirty feet, then began picking their way aft another forty feet.

Every time they brushed their fins on anything, they touched off floury clouds of brown silt. Some of the muck even dislodged when the divers' exhalation bubbles boiled into the warped bulkheads. After more than forty years in the high-pressure environment of the deep, the china closet looked nothing like a closet. Long ago it was cleverly designed to fit under a stairway on the ship. Now it was an open mouth in the rusted steel, the gap shaped like a diamond, the edges like razors. A steel support beam knifed into the corridor; one man could hang on to this while the other propped his elbows on the side of the jagged opening and stretched inside with the rake.

They began to work there. Vince took the rake first. The rake tinkled as he pulled it across the goop inside the closet. It was painstaking. After raking the mud, they had to wait for the silt to settle to see if any china had been unearthed. Out of habit, Murphy glanced frequently at his dive timers. Twelve minutes had passed since he and Vince had entered the water. They wanted to stop the work at the china closet at twenty minutes, which would give them five minutes to back out of the ship and get to the *Seeker's* anchor line.

Vince worked another couple of minutes, then stopped and pointed at Murphy, who took his turn with the rake. Murphy raked the closet down, then waited. Soon a flash of white winked through the soup. It was china.

Murphy reached in and plucked a celery plate. It was intact, and it bore the maroon braids of the first-class service. It was not a cup, or a large dinner plate, but it was boomerang shaped, a bit of an oddity, and he happily placed it in the mesh goodie bag attached to his gear. Time was short, so Murphy thought he'd rake the closet down one more time, as a courtesy to the next team that would inevitably come back to this cache. He began to claw at the muck when Vince reached up to Murphy's mouth and yanked his regulator out of his mouth.

A cloud of bubbles swarmed between them as the regulator released the rest of the air that Murphy had been inhaling.

Stunned, Murphy reached to his left out of a defensive

instinct and grabbed Vince's harness. Keeping Vince at bay in this way, he reached for the emergency regulator hooked to the small bailout canister mounted between the big tanks on his back. He kept that rarely-used regulator clipped up near his right shoulder. In a moment, he had the regulator safely clenched in his mouth. Then he turned to Vince and leaned in so their masks were no more than six inches apart.

Vince pointed at Murphy's back. Murphy didn't understand, so he drew his right index finger across his throat. Using the scuba hand signal for an airflow problem, he was asking Vince whether he was having difficulty breathing. Vince didn't respond.

"You out of air?" Murphy screamed through his mask.

Vince returned a placid gaze. It wasn't clear that he could hear what Murphy was saying.

"You out of air?" Murphy repeated. He pointed at Vince. "You out of air? You out of air?"

Now Vince shook his head furiously. No!

He pointed again at Murphy's back. Now Murphy wondered whether he was the one in trouble. It was possible that his main tanks were leaking. The telltale bubble trail would be invisible to him, but Vince could see it, if that indeed was happening. Is that what Vince meant? If so, could he have chosen a more bizarre and idiotic way of telling Murphy that there was a problem?

Nothing made sense. Murphy wanted out.

"Let's get the fuck out of here!" he screamed.

"Yeah!" Vince replied.

Vince took the lead and they swam out of the wreck. Murphy dropped down to the *Andrea Doria*'s hull as soon as he exited. He needed to get his bearings on the unfamiliar wreck. He also wanted to be on the ship in case he needed to tie off an emergency ascent line. But Vince kept swimming.

Murphy checked the pressure gauges on his main tanks. They indicated that he had plenty of air, even with all the heavy breathing he had just done. He listened for a moment and did- n't hear any hiss from an air leak. His main tanks were fine. He spat out the bailout regulator and replaced it with one from his main tanks. Then he pushed off the mottled skin of the *Andrea Doria*'s hull, and the two men swam aft together—toward the shipwreck's stern.

Murphy stayed within arm's reach of the hull, and Vince swam about twenty-five feet above Murphy. An anchor line appeared, a silken thread in the gloom, and Murphy realized that it belonged to the *Sea Inn*. The *Seeker*'s anchor line was tied higher to the wreck. Vince passed within two feet of the *Sea Inn*'s line and kept swimming. Murphy grabbed the line and planted his feet on the side of the ship. He decided that he might just decompress on the *Sea Inn* line. He didn't know why Vince had continued swim- ming. Did he think the *Seeker*'s anchor line was farther aft? Maybe he wanted to avoid the razzing that greeted any *Andrea Doria* diver who ascended the wrong anchor line.

As Murphy watched, Vince started to slow down.

Murphy let go of the *Sea Inn* line and started after Vince. He saw the familiar pearls pouring from Vince's main tanks. He was breathing. Those were exhaust bubbles. Vince was breathing. But where was he headed? Murphy couldn't put it all together in his mind. He looked at the luminous gauge that told him how long he had been underwater. Eighteen minutes. He needed to get moving to his first decompression stop, which was one hundred feet up the anchor line.

Murphy started to lose sight of Vince.

Dan and Moyer appeared. They were swimming along the ship's length, and Dan had his video camera. At 4:03 P.M., he pointed the lens at Vince, who by now was moving slowly. Vince held his arms straight down, perpendicular to his body. They fluttered, as if they had fallen asleep and he was shaking them to awaken them. His fins moved only inches up and down. He was swimming, at least by the dictionary definition. But it was like a slow-motion film. It would take effort to move your fins that subtly. The two yellow tanks that held Vince's decompression gases hung down on either side of him, and their regulators appeared to be strapped close to those tanks. That was normal. He wouldn't deploy those tanks until he was decompressing on an ascent line.

Faintly illuminated by the brilliant day above, the ocean at the wreck of the *Andrea Doria* was a deep blue-green. Vince swam. The ocean gathered in his form. Murphy watched. He thought Vince was simply checking out some other aspect of the wreck. Maybe. Murphy watched, and Vince's receding image was painted over with successive strokes of green. Then, he was gone.

At 4:08 P.M.—five minutes after Vince was captured swimming lethargically on Dan's video—Nick Caruso stepped from the *Sea Inn*'s cabin, squinted into the afternoon light, and saw a diver in the water fifty feet away. Was the diver adjusting his equipment? Glare bounced off the water. No, he wasn't moving.

Caruso shouted at Tommy Surowiec to retrieve the diver in trouble. Surowiec dived in immediately. He reached the diver and turned his face toward the sky. "I need everyone up here *now*," Caruso said. A few divers, including Santiago Garcia, had been dozing in their bunks below. They all rushed on deck. Caruso threw a line to Surowiec, and they towed in the two men. It wasn't until they got the stricken diver on the *Sea Inn*'s swimming platform, at the boat's stern, that Surowiec recognized the diver as Vince Napoliello.

First they unclipped Vince's main tanks and his decompression stage bottles. Garcia removed Vince's hood. Someone else opened the suit by unzipping the zipper that ran diagonally across the front. They scissored the wrist seals and pulled off Vince's gloves. Surowiec and Caruso began chest compressions and mouth-to-mouth resuscitation. Vince's chest rose a couple of times. His eyes fluttered once. Then his pupils became fixed and dilated. Oddly, for a diver who had apparently risen quickly from a great depth, Vince had none of the froth at his mouth that is associated with a catastrophic lung injury. Maybe he hadn't been that deep when he shot to the surface.

"Hey, Nick, he's got two bottles of 80 percent!" someone shouted.

"Poor bastard, God, look what he did!" another voice said.

Caruso began immediately to think that Vince had succumbed to oxygen toxicity. The cocky *Seeker* crew had failed to catch the slipshod tank labels, and this guy had breathed 80 percent oxygen at a deep-decompression stop—and that was it. The scenario seemed to be torn from the pages of a diving-course textbook.

On the *Seeker*, crew member Pete Wohlleben, a plumbing contractor who was handy with the boat's engines, was resting in his bunk when he heard the shouting from the *Sea Inn*. He watched as the crowd over there lifted someone from the swimming platform to an equipment table under the *Sea Inn*'s long canopy. He rushed up the stairs to the wheelhouse. Jenn Samulski was there. "Is it one of ours, or one of theirs?" he asked.

Several divers were still underwater as the *Sea Inn* crew worked on Vince. Some, such as Steve Gatto, were completing what divers call their decompression "obligations." He was at his ten-foot stop—ten feet below the surface—when he saw a geyser of bubbles climbing from the deep. He knew that it had come from a long way down because they were tiny bubbles, made small by the pressure below. It was the sort of furious bubble cloud made by free-flowing air from a regulator.

Bill Cleary, on the *Seeker*'s anchor line, was deeper in the water at that time, about fifty feet down. He started to think that Vince and Murphy must be also decompressing on the line. A feeling of foreboding suddenly gripped him. He made it to the thirty-foot stop, then, in defiance of logic and training, went back down the anchor line. He could see divers there—at about sixty feet deep—and wondered if it was Vince and Murphy. He got to about forty feet and saw it was Emmett McDowell and Dean Repola. He continued down the line, past those divers, to about seventy feet. He took the regulator out of his mouth so he wouldn't blow out any bubbles. Then he held his breath, hung as far away from the anchor line as he could and peered down into the blue-green void. Again, Cleary felt a tingle of dread.

Cleary resumed his decompression schedule, and at the twenty-foot stop, he saw that a diver with a single tank had popped into the water. Someone obviously had been ordered to do a head count. That confirmed it for Cleary. His instinct had been true. The head counter gave him a thumbs-up, but Cleary couldn't even look at the guy.

On the *Sea Inn*, Caruso asked Joanne Surowiec to examine Vince's equipment. She noticed the inaccurate labels on the decompression tanks, but when she tested the gas in them with a portable analyzer, she found that the mix in one of the bottles was 36 percent oxygen and the mix in the other was 80 percent oxygen. Exactly correct. The 80 percent bottle was, however, only half full. Two possibilities suggested themselves. First, Vince had drained some of the gas in the bottle on his morning dive. Second, he had breathed on the tank—by mistake—on one of his deeper decompression stops and had convulsed from the overpowering oxygen hit.

Joanne Surowiec also tested the isolator valve and found that Vince had apparently dived with it closed.

It seemed, then, that halfway through his dive, Vince's airflow had restricted. All he would have had to do was reach behind his head and open the valve. It was an awkward reach, but divers practiced it constantly. By opening the valve, Joanne Surowiec had opened one door of the ensuing investigation but closed another. As soon as the valve opened, the gas in the full tank flowed into the almost empty tank, and the pressure in the two tanks equalized. So the dregs of air left in the almost empty tank could never be tested. The mix was probably fine. Vince had enjoyed a smooth dive for at least twelve minutes. But without having that gas tested, no one could be sure.

The Coast Guard had been summoned and a helicopter was already on its way. Maritime law required the dive boat crews to maintain rescue breathing until the Coast Guard showed up, and they did.

At 4:56, as the *Sea Inn* crew continued working on Vince, Bill Cleary came out of the water. He had skipped his ten-foot decompression stop because he wanted to tell Dan that he felt something was wrong. He ripped off his mask and saw that members of the *Sea Inn* crew were doing chest compressions on someone.

"Bill, just come into the boat," said a diver, waving him over to the *Seeker*.

"Where is he?" Cleary shouted.

"Bill, just get in the boat."

Cleary started to swim over to the *Sea Inn*. It was about two hundred feet, and such a swim could have been dangerous with all his gear on. A couple of divers in the *Seeker* jumped in the water and herded him back to the *Seeker* ladder.

Two more *Seeker* divers who were helping with the CPR bounced back to the *Seeker* in their inflatable Zodiac. They told Cleary that Vince had heaved to the surface and had no pulse. Another CPR shift of divers prepared to climb down into the Zodiac, to help at the *Sea Inn*, and Cleary tried also to get into the boat. He was losing control. Mike Wagner and Gary Szabo told him he couldn't go because he was too emotional.

Dan emerged from his afternoon dive at 5:03 and the news that Vince was apparently dead rolled into him like a boulder. He was shocked. He had just filmed Vince with his video camera. Had he recorded Vince's last moments? He thought of Craig Sicola. He thought of Richard Roost. Vince had been swimming just one hour earlier. He had just made a video of the

man. He whirled and quickly scanned the decks of the *Seeker*.
Damn it, where was Denis Murphy?

Murphy hit the surface at 5:07 P.M. The *Sea Inn* crew helped
him to their swim platform and turned him away from where
the others were still working on Vince.

"What happened?" Joanne Surowiec asked him.

"I don't know," Murphy replied, apparently believing Joanne
wanted to know why he had ended up on the wrong boat.
"Some kind of problem. We were at 210, working, Vince grabbed
my main reg, I switched over, he said he wasn't out of air, we split.
I lost Vince past the anchor line. I don't know what happened."

"Danny wants you over on the *Seeker*."

The Zodiac zipped over and this time Cleary was aboard.

"Billy, where's Vince?" Murphy asked him.

"Vince popped up," Cleary said, barely composed.

Murphy was relieved. So Vince had shot a inflatable bag and
done an emergency ascent on his own. He had missed the
anchor lines, and that's how he got to the surface.

"No, no. You don't understand," Cleary said, as the Zodiac
turned away from the *Sea Inn*.

"No? What happened?"

"Vince . . . popped up."

Murphy turned his head to look back at the *Sea Inn* and he
realized they were working on Vince on the table. His eyes
began to fill with tears.

The Zodiac nudged along the *Seeker*, and Murphy and Cleary
climbed up to the big boat. Emmett McDowell was now aboard,
having ended his dive at 5:13. He was a police officer in Upper
Saddle River, New Jersey, and a volunteer with the West Milford

first-aid squad. He carried one of his trauma kits from the ambulance corps with him on every diving trip, and Dan knew this. "Emmett," Dan told him, "go over there, if you want to help."

Cleary started to climb down back into the Zodiac.

"Get out of there, Bill," Dan bellowed.

By 5:25 P.M., a Coast Guard helicopter was hovering over the *Sea Inn*. The crew had moved Vince to the bow. A rescue swimmer had been dropped into the water and was now aboard the boat, assisting with placing Vince in the basket that would be lifted to the helicopter. Twenty minutes later, the helicopter left with Vince inside. McDowell came back to the *Seeker* and approached Cleary.

"He's gone," McDowell said.

Dan and the crew prepared the *Seeker* for departure. Three hours of golden summer light remained, but no one wanted to dive anymore.

On the *Sea Inn*, no one felt like diving, either. At least, not until the next morning. The boat remained at the wreck site for two more days. Caruso didn't think there was any reason to cut the trip short. He told people that's what his customers had paid for.

As the afternoon deepened, the sun descended and reddened, and the *Seeker* motored west through calm seas for Montauk. Darkness fell, and Cleary brought up the case of Coronas he had brought to share. He cracked the gold cap from one of the bottles, walked to the side of the boat, and poured it into the water feathering past the hull. "Here, Vince," he said. "This is for you."

Cleary, McDowell, and Dan fired up Arturo Fuentes cigars and settled into spots on the equipment table. As the stars poked through, the sky glistened with what looked like a million broken bits of fine porcelain. Though the night was peaceful, and somber, Dan's head was spinning. Self-doubt was slamming away like a jackhammer. How responsible was he for these deaths? A crack had opened in his stony self-confidence. He wasn't sure that he wanted to be skipper of the *Seeker* anymore. He thought of himself as an artist. He wanted to make underwater films. Hadn't he had his ink drawings of shipwrecks published in magazines and books? He loved scuba diving, but he didn't want to think about other people's diving now. He wasn't sure he should. "Can I stand the emotional strain all this places on me?" he remembered thinking. "I don't know. I don't know."

The men smoked the Dominican cigars quietly in the dark, and they sipped the Coronas, and the *Seeker* took them through the warm night to Montauk.

Seven

DISTRACTIONS

After they told her that Vince had died, Marisa Gengaro searched her apartment for her microcassette recorder and called his office in Manhattan.

As soon as Vince's machine started to answer, she pushed PLAY and RECORD on the recorder.

"Hi," said Vince's voice. "I'm either on the phone or I'm not in. Leave a message and I'll get back to you as soon as I can."

Then she went her bed and lay down and listened to the message over and over. It was dark in the apartment. Outside, the orange light of the street lights washed the cluster of high-rise apartment buildings like a sulfurous sea.

She unhooked the phone and lay there in the dark. "Hi, I'm either on the phone or I'm not in. Leave a message and I'll get back to you as soon as I can."

Her apartment had a lot of Vince's things. He kept his humidor on a living room table, packed with good-brand cigars such as Tabantilla and Gran Reserva and Arturo Fuentes. Because Vince was studying for his Coast Guard's captain's license—to re able boatsman, not to work commercially— igation and maritime rules sat stacked in the cor- lay of photos on a bookshelf, Marisa and Vince edding and Vince, with a ball cap turned backward, nd black sunglasses, held a bottle of Corona. In her d a tub of *Andrea Doria* china, Vince's souvenirs from ip to the wreck with Bill Cleary. He hadn't gotten around yet to cleaning the cache. It smelled of worm-grouted wood, microscopic organisms drying out, and oil.

Someone had called her from the boat, asking her if she had heard the news. No, she had not, what? She could hear the *Seeker*'s thrumming engines in the background. Later, one of her brothers had come to her door on the eleventh floor with the confirmation. "Vincent's drowned," was all he could say. The words played over and over in her head. "Vincent's drowned, Vincent's drowned."

When she couldn't stand it, she played her little tape recording from the message machine.

Coast Guard Lieutenant Tim Dickerson was on a ferryboat headed across Long Island Sound when he learned of Vince's death. He and others from the safety office were traveling to a meeting at the Coast Guard office in Coram, Long Island. He was stunned, and he struggled to understand why three men had been killed within several weeks of one another, and all from the same charter boat, the *Seeker*. There was no body to meet at the dock this time, so he didn't send an investigator. But statements had to be collected and the dead diver's equipment impounded. He asked the Coast Guard station in Montauk to meet the *Seeker*. The boat arrived at about 7:30 the next morning.

Bill Cleary's charter to the *Andrea Doria* had been the last scheduled expedition to the wreck that summer, so Dan then took the *Seeker* back out around Montauk Point, south across the Atlantic Ocean channel between New York and New Jersey known as the New York Bight, and to the marina at Manasquan Inlet. He had charters already booked for dive sites closer than the *Andrea Doria* to the Jersey shore, but he was not enthusiastic. He continued to wonder whether he could have done anything to prevent the three deaths. Vince's death bothered him the most because of the three men who had died, he knew Vince best. He appreciated Vince's style. Vince also had the respect of diver and explorer John Chatterton, and there were few people Dan respected as much as he did the well-spoken Chatterton. Vince had no false machismo, thought Dan, just a businesslike competence with the tanks, the air mixes and all that extra safety gear he liked to talk about.

From some of the evidence, Dan believed, it seemed Vince had suffered some kind of catastrophic internal injury while diving the *Doria*, and if that were the case, then how could it have been avoided? A natural cause of death for Vince would, in the harsh logic of the circumstances, reassure Dan. But if it was true that Vince's isolator valve was closed, that led to questions about how well he had been trained.

Dan had not trained Vince for Trimix diving, but questions about training and the industry's certification process, such as it was, invited government agencies such as the Coast Guard to scrutinize. It also gave ammunition to the dinosaurs like Steve Bielenda and the know-nothings and the non-divers, including virtually every reporter he had ever met. The non-divers seemed to think he was, or should be, some sort of helpful trail guide to the deep. They had no idea of the idiosyncratic nature of every diver's gear configuration, how big the egos were, how the only people he could ever "guide" were the true first-timers—and even the majority of those guys had years of experience.

Dan thought of himself as a bus driver. The best bus driver, of course, but, really, just a bus driver. Dan had completely

understood when Denis Murphy had sworn on the ride back to
Montauk that he wanted to burn all his diving gear. Ten thousand
dollars in equipment, up in smoke. He empathized. But he also felt
strongly that every accident had an explanation. The wreck of the
Andrea Doria was not cursed, as some of the newspaper headlines
suggested. Lust for china was not killing the divers of the *Seeker*. You
had to do "accident analysis," the divers called it. So he searched for
explanations. He analyzed the accident. He offered the ideas to the
Coast Guard. He certainly felt they had no idea what they were
doing. And, all along, what stabilized Dan, what shored him up in
the storm of questions, besides talking to a friend such as
Chatterton—who supported him and knew the feeling of having
dead divers on deck—who had been running the *Seeker* with him
in 1992 when diver Chrissy Rouse had died, was the unyielding
demand of the *Seeker's* charter schedule. People had made deposits.
These amounted to contracts for his professional services. He was
forty years old now. He couldn't just bail out. He had not killed
anyone. Deep wreck diving carried an inherent risk, and it said that
right on the release form every *Seeker* diver signed. Emotionally, he
told people he felt "hammered." It was the same word he used for
feeling drunk. He was disoriented, but he was not falling apart. He
had bills to pay, and he paid them by driving the bus.

At the wake for Vince a couple of days later, Denis Murphy
remained in a sort of trance. On the trip back to Montauk, he
had told the other *Seeker* divers that he wanted to get out of
diving. His mind had already edited a swirl of dreamy impres-
sions to a few selected for particularly disturbing qualities: He
and Vince swim furiously out of the ship, their bodies bathed in
clouds of exhalation bubbles and, later, Vince's silhouette shrinks

slowly behind the green shroud of the deep ocean. One moment repeated itself in Murphy's mind: He and Vince are face-to-face, and Murphy is screaming, "Are you all right?" and Vince returns the stare, dazed and uncomprehending.

At Vince's wake, Murphy met John Chatterton. He'd known Chatterton only by the celebrity he enjoyed among divers as the man who had finally identified the *U-869*. A diver who finds and identifies a new shipwreck is like an archaeologist hitting upon an undiscovered tomb. As in so many other endeavors, it was original work in scuba diving that built reputations. Chatterton and Dan were old friends, both former crew members of the original *Seeker* skipper, Bill Nagle.

He and Murphy talked in the parking lot at the funeral home. Murphy told the whole story. Chatterton had done some checking around, had satisfied himself that Murphy was an accomplished, careful diver, and he shared this with Murphy. He told Murphy that if he wanted to continue diving, he needed to get back into the water as soon as possible. "You understand, just like we all do," he told Murphy, "if you can help the other person when something like this happens, great, but we all know, even if you're diving with someone else, you're really diving with yourself."

Chatterton had articulated the stark and unforgiving code of the technical wreck divers. Ultimately, few of them would blame a fellow diver for looking out for himself. After all, the whole idea behind the costly assemblage of a gloriously redundant scuba rig—the multiple regulators, lights, knives, and air tanks— was to make yourself a self-contained, self-rescuing underwater swimming machine. While Murphy appreciated the philosophical nature of Chatterton's friendly advice, he had already decided to dive again, eventually. But he was not sure whether he wanted to dive again with a partner. Maybe it would be best, he reasoned, if he felt responsible for no one except himself. He could not escape the feeling that he should never have let go of Vince when they had that exchange of words down at the china hole. He had Vince by the equipment harness, and he should have never let go. He felt like the person who is keeping a bedside vigil for a sick relative, then ducks out for a meal only to return to learn the relative has died. There's an illogical feeling of responsibility there, as if the person has caused the death.

These were Murphy's feelings, and no one in diving would have blamed him if he'd decided that he would dive solo. It went, of course, against all diving-safety tenets. Craig Sicola was alone when he died, and so was Richard Roost. But the divers were not doctrinaire. They felt they had trained in many ways beyond the rules.

For all that had happened to Denis Murphy at the *Andrea Doria*, he also resolved to return to the wreck. He said he had demons to exorcise. He knew this sounded unbelievable but it was the way he felt, and this was what weighed upon his mind every day: "My own little demons," he called them. It was an empty feeling in the pit of his stomach and it would not go away, he believed, until he was once again diving the wreck. He hungered for a clean and uneventful dive at the *Doria*.

As the hot summer ebbed and the mild days of September took hold in the Northeast, the *Seeker* made news. The Associated Press had picked up on the Napoliello story immediately, though its reporter had not reached Dan. *The Cape Cod Times* also published a story. Still, no comment from Dan. A reporter for *The Record* in Hackensack, where Cleary had his office, began to prepare an in-depth series of stories. Finally Dan found himself quoted directly about the deaths. The article appeared on page 57 in the *Newsday*, the daily newspaper distributed on Long Island. Veteran writer Bill Bleyer, who is also an avid recreational diver, got Dan on the telephone. Vince "may have run out of gas and inadvertently grabbed" the wrong tank, Dan told Bleyer. "He maybe used the wrong mix at depth, which would create oxygen toxicity and he probably would have convulsed and passed out."

The Coast Guard had worked on a public statement to address issues raised by the death of the three men. Glen Rosenholm, a spokesman for the Coast Guard's First District, which covered the Northeast, told a series of reporters that divers needed to make sure their equipment was in good working order; they needed to have the right level of experience before they explored a deep wreck such as the *Andrea Doria*; and they should always dive with a partner. Rosenholm didn't know if anyone had suffered equipment failures. Rosenholm also acknowledged that the Coast Guard had no mechanism to ensure that its recommended safety practices were followed. For-profit training agencies, which offered certification courses for scuba divers, set the standards. There was no government oversight whatsoever.

Rosenholm said the Coast Guard was not even required to probe the deaths at the *Andrea Doria*. "There is not a federal agency that regulates recreational diving. In fact, the *Andrea Doria* is in international waters. We have no regulatory jurisdiction in this case actually. We do regulate commercial charter boats like the *Seeker* and how they operate and what types of safety equipment that they have on board, but divers who dive on the *Andrea Doria* are not subject per se to those regulations."

Down in Brick, New Jersey, where he and Jenn lived, Dan started to give a few telephone tutorials to reporters on the intricacies of deep diving and the history of the local charter operations. While he placed the blame for the deaths that summer on the divers themselves (Craig, Vince maybe) or on unforeseen medical emergencies (Richard), he was also clearly affected by the incidents. He constantly replayed the fatal dives in his mind. He attended a wedding in the late summer and could not put Vince out of his mind because he knew Vince and Marisa were to have been married the following spring. He wanted to know if he could have done something, anything, differently. In the devastation, he wanted to see whether there was something important to be learned.

He exuded less of the Hollywood bravado that seems to mark so many of the Jersey and Long Island divers. For them, it was an "expedition" every time they pushed away from the dock. Dan's style was cooler, ironic. He voiced a dismissive attitude about the dangers of deep wreck diving, yet he was strangely humble. He even acknowledged that he would be unnerved if he had attempted the path through the *Doria* chosen by Craig Sicola. "I would be a little nervous. You can get into as much trouble as you want to on the *Doria*. That's always been the problem with this kind of wreck. The *Doria* will give you everything you need to get into a shitload of trouble."

Dan and Jennifer Samulski shared a raised ranch house on a leafy street in the coastal village of Brick. The minimal landscaping—a thick carpet of pine needles—is that of residents who spend most of their time at home indoors. They got enough fresh air aboard their boat. The garage door was as often open as closed, and Dan could often be found in there, repairing diving equipment. He stands about six feet tall, with a tapered physique and thick forearms. He doesn't look as though he works with weights to bulk up; he looks as if he does hard physical work all the time.

The neatly kept house was not only where Dan and Jenn lived, it was the corporate offices of Deep Explorers, Inc. From there, they marketed diving charters, underwater videos, and diving instruction. Their home felt like a sort of stationary extension of the *Seeker*. Floor to ceiling, the garage is as well stocked as any dive shop: Air tanks and masks and dry suits and odd lengths of steel piping and lanyards and lights and fins were everywhere. Five Rubbermaid tubs held china taken from the *Andrea Doria*. There were thirty-two demitasse cups and exactly one hundred saucers.

Upstairs, in the living room of the home, Dan had a custom-built table box in which were arranged six polished pieces of officers' china from the *Andrea Doria*, each bearing a single red band around the edge. The box also held a richly colored piece of costume jewelry he took from the wreck. It was a bracelet, a silver braid securing a sapphire-blue gemstone ringed by eight gold flowers. The staterooms of the *Andrea Doria* are in most cases beyond the scuba divers, but the ship's gift shop, on the Foyer Deck, has proven to be the source of many trinkets over the years. The deterioration of the ship has meant that many of these items, once displayed under glass, have dropped to unexpected places in the wreck. Dan found the bracelet on a crumpled beam one day.

Few people have ever retrieved anything like it from the wreck. *Andrea Doria* divers talk a lot about helping non-divers get a feeling for the age of the ocean liners with the artifacts they bring up from the wreck, but their piles of plates and stacks of cutlery do not much convey the experience of the passenger. Diners on the *Andrea Doria* did not see china in piles. They saw it only as carefully arranged elements of the place settings laid out by stewards of the Italian Line. The silver bracelet, however, was different. It evoked life aboard the *Andrea Doria*. In this way, the bracelet was like the old records Gary Gentile had once lifted from the wreck; here was the music people danced to in the 1950s as they crossed the ocean. If the voyage had not been interrupted, the bracelet might have been a gift given with intention, something slipped on and then perhaps admired in the evening by starlight streaming through the windows of the Belvedere Lounge.

Downstairs in his home in Brick, Dan had a complete video suite. He had monitors, an editing station, and underwater video cameras. His prize camera was the VH 1000 Amphibico. On the wall was Dan's original pen-and-ink drawing of the *U-869*. A map of Northeast wrecks covered another wall, and nautical charts lay rolled on a shelf. In the videotape shot during the dives that summer, carefree undersea images were interwoven with documentary shots of the body recoveries: A leatherneck turtle paddles peacefully past a diver, then the body of Richard Roost is hauled aboard the *Seeker* on the boat's davit like an ungainly clam cage.

Dan spent time reviewing his best tape of Richard Roost. The diver from Michigan appeared rumpled in cargo shorts and a blue turtleneck. He looked with tired eyes toward Dan and

Gary Gentile, who were using toothbrushes to shine the china they had recovered from the wreck below.

The video captured the *Seeker* crew responding with calm and professionalism to the emergencies. Voices sounded clipped, and responses were usually offered in just a word or two, but the speedy organization of the attempted rescues and body recoveries was impressive. "You're actually feeling a lot of emotions as you do all this stuff," Dan said. "You get really mad at every one of the guys who's missing. You think they did something stupid."

When he wasn't working at home, Dan was in Brielle, where the *Seeker* was docked at the Harbor Inn Marina. Next to the dirt parking lot and on the dock lay a rusty, knocked-over object about the dimensions of a upright gasoline pump. It was the *Andrea Doria*'s "gyro pilot."

It was a piece of automatic-steering equipment that once stood bolted down in the bridge of the ship. In the 1950s, it represented the most advanced ship-steering equipment aboard any ocean liner in the world. Although the gyro pilot was an intriguing bit of nautical machinery taken from a ship that, after all, had sunk as a result of navigational error, it was difficult to see why the *Andrea Doria* divers had bothered to bring the thing up from the depths.

Unlike so many other artifacts, no one was restoring the gyro pilot, or selling it online, or storing it in temperature-controlled sheds. If the *Andrea Doria* was an underwater museum, as the divers claimed while they retrieved their china and other, more portable trophies, the old gyro was an artifact for which they cared little. It was left simply to disintegrate in the sea air of Manasquan.

⚓ ⚓ ⚓

In September, Dan left for Greece, where he and Jenn were assisting a team of largely British divers set to explore the wreck of the HHS *Britannic*. The logistics of this trip, and the preparation for the planned dives to 390 feet deep (an extraordinary depth for scuba divers, twice as deep as the top of the sunken *Andrea Doria*) helped Dan muck through the stressful weeks following the summer of 1998. It was a relief for him to not be in charge of everything for once. He also escaped the media questions, which had been posed not just by American reporters, but also by the BBC, *The Sunday Telegraph* in London, and the *Frankfurter Allgemeine* in Germany. He would also slip away from the hot-house atmosphere that had settled on the Northeast diving community, a stultifying air of mourning and gossip and second-guessing. He liked to say he always looked forward, not back, and what was billed as the "HHS *Britannic* 98 Technical Diving Expedition" was an enormous venture before him.

British diver Nick Hope had negotiated for two years with the Greek government to gain access to the dive site, which lay forty miles southeast of Athens, in the Aegean Sea. Dan would serve as an "expedition support diver." Jenn would provide topside logistic support, the same role she played on *Seeker* charters. She would note divers' times in and out, their breathing gas, and other record-ing duties that are critical to the proper and safe organization of such complex dive operations. Dan's pal John Chatterton would also go along. Although the stated aim of the expedition (and this was a genuine expedition) was to learn more about the cause of the *Britannic*'s sinking on November 21, 1916—a German mine was suspected—the primary objective was to simply document the wreck's modern-day condition. Unlike the *Andrea Doria* wreck, the *Britannic* was not picked over and the exact circumstances of its demise remained mysterious. While perhaps a thousand people had dived on the *Doria*, the club of twenty or so divers who had used scuba to explore the *Britannic* wreck had a more rarefied air about it. To give the project the cachet of a nation-sponsored adventure, such as when climbers are sponsored for an Everest expedition, claims were hyped about "*Britannic* 98" representing the first visit to the site by a team of divers, and marking the first time a woman had ever dived on the great wreck.

Dan didn't make such claims. For him, *Britannic* 98 was simply a thrilling technical challenge, an unusually deep dive on a fabled liner. Instead of traditional scuba tanks, Dan would make the dives using a rebreather—a backpacklike device that cleans and recirculates air to breathe underwater. Rebreathers emit none of the comforting exhalation bubbles so closely associated with scuba diving. For this reason, the quiet machines unnerve many divers. But Dan was a technology aficionado who prided himself on using his sport's cutting-edge gear. Many in the industry predict that one day everyone will dive with rebreathers.

While the *Titanic* rests in more than five thousand feet of seawater, well beyond scuba, the *Britannic* is within reach for highly skilled divers. The weather was rough for the expedition, but Dan still managed to squeeze in three dives. Using the Amphibico camera, he made images of the other team members descending on the wreck. His best day was September 20, when he dropped almost to the spot where the *Britannic*'s bow section had slammed into the sand after the explosion. The tip of the bow now rested just twelve inches above the seabed. Later, exhilarated, he typed an entry into divers' logs: "Though much of the railing is crumpled, the flag pole stands straight out, undamaged."

The same month that Dan plunged to more than 350 feet at the historic wreck of the *Britannic*, Cincinnati businessman Christopher Murley dived to eighty feet near in Dale Hollow Lake, in northern Tennessee.

Murley had been diving for seven months. He had decided to learn how to dive when he won a trip to Hawaii as an award for selling a lot of business telephone systems. He became hooked. He'd had other obsessions—restoring muscle cars, collecting guns—but nothing had captivated him like scuba diving. He stood six feet eight inches and weighed anywhere from 320 to 350 pounds, so he had to get a letter from his doctor before he began training.

The twenty-seven-acre Dale Hollow Lake had been created in 1944. The U.S. Army Corps of Engineers dammed sixty-one miles of the Obey River in the Cumberland Mountains and built a dam to produce hydroelectric power. The inundation of the valley had necessitated the destruction of an old mountain community, Willow Grove, and Midwestern divers such as Chris enjoyed poking around the underwater ruins there. Wood-framed windows of the Willow Grove Schoolhouse remained intact at the bottom of the clear blue lake.

Chris managed only fifty-four seconds of bottom time before he cut the dive short. He did not feel well. Even as Dan Crowell took a needed step back from the world of the *Andrea Doria*, Chris was in pursuit of his ambitious goal of diving on the *Doria* the following summer.

He had been diving for less than one year, and he had conducted most of his training dives at Gilboa Quarry, near Cincinnati. He had let it slip that his goal at the *Andrea Doria* was to somehow unbolt a toilet and bring it back to Ohio, where he and his fiancée, Mary Beth Byrne, wanted to add a room to their house and stock it with diving treasures and memorabilia.

The couple had met at the annual Christmas party thrown the year before by the High Cincinnatians Tall Club, a social organization that required its women members to be at least five feet ten inches tall and men to be six foot two. Mary Beth was six-two and wearing a red dress that night. Chris asked the DJ to play "Lady in Red" and they had been inseparable since. Between them they had five divorces: Chris had been married three times previously and Mary Beth twice. They were both forty-four years old and felt they had finally found the right person.

Mary Beth went along with Chris's toilet idea because she saw how much fun he had diving. Chris had a way of not hearing people who asked him how he would find the toilet inside the ship, unbolt it, and raise it to the surface of the ocean. He had no experience in marine salvage.

Dan did not know Chris Murley, but he knew that Chris's instructor, Joe Jackson, planned to charter the *Seeker* the following summer for two trips to the wreck of the *Andrea Doria*.

The aborted dive at the Dale Hollow dam marked Chris's thirty-first dive since he'd begun logging his open-water dives the previous March. A couple of weeks later, on October 5, Chris filled out an "Experience Summary" page in his diving log. The page categorized Chris's dives, according to whether he made them in fresh or salt water, from the shore or from a boat, in a current or in surf, at night, whether they required him to ascend with decompression stops, and whether they were deep dives of more than sixty feet.

A dive to the *Andrea Doria* would combine all the toughest elements of open-water diving. A diver there contended with a current, with ascending the dive boat's ladder, with the required decompression. Whereas Chris's log noted that he had made forty-three dives overall in the previous six months, Dan had made three times that number of dives to the *Andrea Doria* alone. Chris's schedule appeared to chart the progress of someone learning as much as he could about the sport in the shortest possible time.

Chris was a fast learner and well equipped, but to skeptics, he personified the "patch diver" who substituted a sleeve's length of embroidered certification patches for years of experience in the water.

Chris's log broke down his experience in this way:

FRESH WATER: 22

SALT WATER: 21

SHORE : 27

BOAT: 16

CURRENT: 16

SURF: 5

NIGHT DIVES: 2

DEEP DIVES: 16

DECOMPRESSION: 2

OVER 200 FEET: 2

Eight

ACCIDENT ANALYSES

One day in February 1999, William Murley walked into his son's office in the Cincinnati suburb of Woodlawn only to find Chris lying down on the floor. His eyes were closed, and his clothes were drenched in perspiration head to toe.

Closing the door so Chris's employees at Better Telephones & Technology would not see Chris prostrate, the elder Murley asked his son what was going on.

"I don't know what it is," Chris murmured. "I just—this just happens to me."

Chris said he suffered from headaches, deep fatigue and prodigious sweating. Sometimes he just sweated. Other times all the symptoms flared at once, and he had to lower his huge frame to the floor and lie down. He told his father that a doctor had advised him he might have the early signs of diabetes. On the doctor's advice, Chris had begun watching his diet. He was trying to keep sugary foods to a minimum.

As Chris lay there, the conversation came around to his scuba diving training, and his stated goal of diving on the *Andrea Doria*. Chris's father opposed the dive. It was clear to him his son was ill. William Murley, seventy-four, had served twenty-four years in the U.S. Army and, as a paratrooper, had made five combat jumps over Korea. He liked to say that, in the jump planes, if the officers sensed a paratrooper was even subtly unprepared, or uncertain, or sick, they would cancel the soldier's jump at a moment's notice. To him, it was obvious Chris was not 100 percent. His son had been walking around for two years with his clothes plastered to his body with perspiration.

The old paratrooper also frequently made the point that the air was unforgiving—he meant the air between the troop plane and the ground. He felt the same way about the water. The environment allowed for very few errors. William Murley had a gut feeling. His son shouldn't go to the *Andrea Doria*.

Chris rested on the floor. His father asked him if he could get up, and he said no.

"I'll be all right," he said.

The two men had drawn close in the previous six or seven years. Chris's father had a little income-tax preparation business in the Better Telephones & Technology building, which was located on the Springfield Pike between Dayton and Cincinnati. William Murley, who had earned two college degrees during his time in the military, followed his career in uniform with eighteen years as an auditor at the General Accounting Office, and helped his son run the phone business. It wasn't working out very well. The corporation lost more than $130,000 in 1997 and more than $150,000 the year before. Nevertheless, the passage of time had partially healed some deep wounds between the two men. It had been especially hard on William Murley when his son, who had been enrolled in the Reserve Officers' Training Corps in college, went on active duty only to be court-martialed and convicted for theft of government property and conduct unbecoming an officer, among other charges. Chris even served six months in 1982 at the government's Military Disciplinary Barracks at Fort Leavenworth, Kansas, and was dishonorably discharged. In 1999, Chris had been working with the government to get his discharge status upgraded.

Now, as they talked in Chris's office, William Murley tried to persuade him to abandon his strange obsession with diving the *Andrea Doria*. He asked his son if he was satisfied with his diving. Chris said he was, until he got "in trouble." The equipment and the techniques weren't always easy to master. Murley remembers finally asking his son not to go the *Doria*.

"You know you're sick," he said.

"I'm committed," Chris said. "I've got money tied up in this. I can't back out on it. It's a noncancelable contract."

William Murley suggested that the *Doria* dive was simply beyond his son's abilities. Chris, his father recalled, said that was OK. He'd be qualified for it when he returned.

"Pursuant to our telephone conversation of Feb. 4, 1999, I am sending you this video tape of Vince Napoliello taken prior to his surfacing Aug. 4, 1998 which resulted in his death. As you view the tape you will see that both of Vince's stage bottles are hanging down below him (one on either side) and that the hoses to the regulators are still strapped to the bottles, which would make it highly improbable that he could breathe from either regulator in this configuration."

Coast Guard Lieutenant Tim Dickerson read the letter in his office in New Haven. Outside there was a white winter sky, and the western reaches of Long Island Sound were ashen. It was late afternoon, and the Coast Guard office was sleepy. Earlier, in the Marine Safety Office where he worked, Dickerson had been typing an inspection report for a commercial boat he had

boarded that week. Radio chatter from harbor pilots and tug-
boat skippers buzzed over little speakers mounted in offices
throughout the brick building.

At the top of the letter to Dickerson was the word "*Seeker.*"
The letter, dated six months from the day that Vince died, was
from Dan Crowell. It distilled Dan's effort to explain what had
happened to Vince. After Dan had returned from Greece, he
learned that Vince had occlusive coronary artery disease, or
hardening of the arteries in the heart. A physician with the
Massachusetts state medical examiner's office in Barnstable,
where Vince's body was taken after the Coast Guard chopper
evacuated him, had made note of Vince's heart disease in his
autopsy report on January 23. In characterizing the heart disease, Dr. James Weiner noted that Vince had "severe" blockage
of the left descending coronary artery.

These facts fit neatly with Dan's instinct about Vince—that he
was a competent scuba diver felled by a catastrophic medical
emergency. Vince's training therefore could not be questioned.
The exhausted Richard Roost, wearied from the long drive from
the Midwest and then beaten up by the elements at sea, had fall-
en asleep underwater. Vince's heart troubles helped Dan construct
his latest accident analysis.

"I don't believe that Vince used either stage bottle and the
video is clear in showing that fact. With evidence that shows
Vince's coronary artery to be obstructed, I believe the CO_2
buildup within Vince's tissues occurred due to the lack of blood
flow as a result of the obstruction. This would decrease [profu-
sion] of gas to and from the tissues thereby retarding the elimi-
nation of CO_2 or the uptake of oxygen. The increased levels of

CO_2 along with the lack of oxygen is what I believe is the reason for Vince's incapacitation."

Dan's was an impressive analysis, and while it had the ring of probability, not all of it was indisputably true and its conclusions were impossible to prove. Dan's analysis couldn't be dismissed, however. He had years of experience and had witnessed some of the events. But his breezy confidence about what exactly had occurred was hardly justified. There were gaps in the sequence of events. It might have been that he did not see all that had occurred.

Dr. Weiner listed "asphyxia by drowning" as the cause of death, along with "other significant conditions" such as oxygen toxicity and the heart disease. Drowning was the cause of death in most scuba fatalities, and Weiner had told the Coast Guard he had listed oxygen toxicity based on his reading of an investigatory report submitted by Terrence Cunningham, deputy police chief for the town of Wellesley, Massachusetts. Cunningham's analysis, like Dan's, could not be discounted, for the deputy chief had remarkable credentials for a small-town police official. He was a top-level scuba diver and had dived several times on the wreck of the *Andrea Doria*. With about the same information as Dan, Cunningham had puzzled together a different scenario.

Vince's bizarre behavior inside the wreck, when he ripped Murphy's regulator from his mouth, was the most mysterious aspect of the series of events that led to his death. Cunningham concluded that Vince may have had difficulty drawing air from his double set of tanks because his isolator valve may have been shut down. Some technical divers close this valve when they dive and, when they begin to exhaust the air in one tank, they reach behind their heads and twist open the knob.

Most divers do not do this, however. Vince did not, according to his dive buddies. Like other divers who want to make certain the valve is open, Vince was known to shut the knob down, then crack it back open. That was the only way to know if it was open—by closing it briefly, then reopening.

Cunningham believed Vince dived with his isolator valve closed. It could explain the sudden panic Vince exhibited and his rush to get out of the wreck. It may be that panic so overwhelmed Vince that he believed he was completely without air. Cunningham believed that after swimming out of view of Murphy, John Moyer, and Dan Crowell, Vince grabbed one of his decompression stop regulators and sucked a fatal hit of oxygen-rich gas. Under this scenario, Vince then convulsed and drowned.

Even Cunningham's construction relied upon a substantial number of unknowns. No one knew what happened after 4:03 P.M. on August 4; that was the last time Vince had been caught on Dan's camera. His was barely pumping his diving fins, his arms were hanging down, and his hands fluttered. These could have been symptoms of one form of oxygen toxicity known as central nervous system toxicity; his slow, straight swimming suggested someone experiencing tunnel vision.

Murphy, hunched down on the wreck, lost sight of Vince. Even allowing for another minute to pass, four full minutes remained between the last time anyone saw Vince and the moment his body was spotted as it heaved to the surface. It seemed like sufficient time for him to grab a decompression regulator and draw air from it.

The crew of the *Sea Inn* claimed that they saw that Vince had deployed one of the regulators on one of his decompression air bottles when they brought him, almost lifeless, aboard their boat. Nick Caruso was especially emphatic.

But Caruso was often emphatic. Unlike Dan, he did not modulate his comments on practically anything. Whereas Dan's accident analysis, however incomplete, sounded reasonable coming from his mouth, Caruso's scenario, probably as likely as Dan's, sounded like a testy argument. Although Caruso said he respected Dan, and admired the business he had built, he was no fan of the *Seeker*. He didn't think people on the rival boat watched out for each other. He felt the *Seeker* received an inordinate amount of attention; he and his Sea Dwellers customers aboard the *Sea Inn* had performed CPR on Vince for more than two hours, yet the Coast Guard had never called to ask him about the case. Meanwhile, Dan and Lieutenant Dickerson were e-mail pals. It grated on Nick Caruso. "The egos on that boat cause deaths," he said. "I've seen it. Basically, when you go on that boat, there's no camaraderie. Before someone on my vessel rolls into the water, myself or one of the crew is going to thoroughly check out the diver and his equipment."

Nick had a terrier's intensity about him, and so when his chance came to try to embarrass Dan about the deaths of Sicola, Roost, and Napoliello, he lunged at it.

It came in March 1999 at Beneath the Sea, the sprawling diving and travel convention held annually in Secaucus, New Jersey. Beneath the Sea is all things to all people in the recreational diving industry. Vendors hawk training courses, diving equipment, and scuba-travel packages to clear-water destinations such as the Bahamas and Cozumel. The various training agencies have booths there, which adds an official air to the show, with their banners and logos that involve a graphic image of a gridded Earth and a double set of air tanks. Visitors alternate between the rubbery forests of merchandise and several seminar rooms, where the sport's eminences hold forth on underwater photography, advanced-diving techniques, and shipwreck exploration.

Dan was there to deliver a presentation on the diving deaths at the *Andrea Doria*. He wore a necktie and sport coat and looked pinched. The large seminar room reserved for his talk was packed fifteen minutes before he started. When he began talking, people were sitting cross-legged in the aisles. Nick Caruso was standing in the rear of the room.

Dan showed a video that included some of the television interviews he had given during the previous several months. Steve Bielenda was in the front row. Dan was a bit stiff on the stump and Steve helped him along by tossing out convenient questions. Bielenda asked about the causes of death of the men who had died the previous summer.

"Craig Sicola, embolism. Richard Roost, drowning. Vince Napoliello . . . I don't know if the M.E. [medical examiner] has a whole hell of a lot of experience in this."

He did not go into the medical examiner's official conclusion that Vince had drowned and that he had suffered oxygen toxicity.

Then Caruso piped up from the back in a loud voice. He introduced himself and suggested that Vince had indeed succumbed to oxygen toxicity.

"Which" Dan interrupted, inaccurately, "has already been ruled out."

Caruso then talked about Vince's mislabeled tanks and suggested that Dan's crew had been lax in not insisting that Vince label the bottles correctly. Dan responded that the bottles had been tested and both contained precisely what Vince had claimed they did. What was the problem?

Caruso felt that mistakes happened on the *Seeker* because people were topping off their gas bottles and forgetting what was in them, and—in Vince's case—breathing from the wrong air tank.

"Don't you think it would be a better policy—safer—to eliminate gas blending on the *Seeker*?"

Chairs squeaked. People in the audience were swiveling to get a look at the guy in the back with the Sea Dwellers T-shirt and ponytail. Caruso's chiseling questions seemed so far to have produced few sparks.

Again, Dan shrugged and said no. He was convinced Vince knew the contents of each decompression bottle. Even if Vince had breathed from the wrong bottle—and Dan did not believe that had happened—it wasn't a mistake due to labeling.

Divers at this level were not checking the tank labels before they breathed on them. They had everything rigged so they could operate in the dark if necessary. They knew on which side of their rig they customarily carried their 36 percent oxygen tank and on which side they carried their 80 percent. For them, grabbing the regulators was a practiced motion, like a champion cyclist reaching down and unclipping a water bottle from a moving bicycle's frame.

"Look," said Dan, scratching his head from his hairline to the back of his head, as if he were combing out some dust that had settled there, "if you're qualified to mix gas, you can blend it on my boat. And, look, I'm not everyone's leader out there, okay? It's not my responsibility to baby-sit all these people."

Bielenda stood up. He was also no baby-sitter. It's the divers' responsibility to check their own gas, and recheck any blends they do on the dive boat, he said. It was that simple. Each diver, he liked to say, was under his or her own "custody and control."

Caruso, the terrier, kept gnawing.

"I feel the Vince Napoliello thing could have been something that would not have happened if he hadn't blended gas on that boat," he said.

"Well, I don't really want to go over the whole deal here, now, but yes, the tanks were mismarked, and we'll have stronger policies this season to address that," Dan said. "But basically the conversation is moot now as far as Vince Napoliello goes. Like I said earlier, he had blocked arteries and I think Vince just basically had a heart attack while he was at the wreck."

Bielenda again stood up. He looked pointedly at the back of the room, where Nick Caruso stood arms folded across his chest. Caruso could be so polarizing that he could make Bielenda a defender of his rival, Dan. "The Monday-morning quarterbacking," Bielenda said, "is hard without all the facts."

Caruso did not respond.

Afterward, as he loosened his necktie, Dan rolled his eyes when asked about Caruso's argument. He felt sure no one would take Caruso seriously. "Hey, that really is a consider-the-source kind of deal, you know what I mean?"

Yet Dan had said he would institute new policies on gas

blending for the coming season. Dan was hardly in retreat. He had scheduled eleven charters to the *Doria* for the upcoming summer. But he had been openly challenged in public by Nick Caruso, and there was no guarantee that the people in the seminar room knew of what Dan perceived as Caruso's crude biases.

And Dan had also just acknowledged that the operation aboard the Seeker was not as safe as it could be. What had just happened was not good for business.

Around this time, dive instructor Joel Silverstein found himself in Columbus, Ohio, at a big scuba conference. For several years, Silverstein had published *Sub Aqua Journal,* a defunct but respected diving magazine. Over the years, he had helped operate hyperbaric centers, where divers with decompression illness could be helped, and he was an executive with a company that made high-end equipment specifically designed for technical divers. Silverstein had dived on the Andrea Doria forty-six times, and he planned to make it an even fifty. After his talk ended, Silverstein was approached by the biggest man in the room. It was Christopher Murley, who had started diving one year previously and who now told Silverstein he aimed to explore the famed wreck during the upcoming summer.

"Well," said Silverstein, surprised the man would be approaching the *Andrea Doria* at such an early stage in his career. "How are you feeling about that?"

"My instructor feels I'm ready," Murley said.

"Well, how do *you* feel?"

"I feel I should have all my training dives in by then."

Silverstein walked away from the brief conversation disturbed.

The diver he had just spoken with had virtually no ocean-diving experience. He had been diving for one year. Murley issued no affirmative declaration—Yes, I'm ready! Finally! I can do it. It was strange.

To Joel Silverstein, there was something not quite right with Chris Murley.

Nine

SIX-EIGHT, THREE TWENTY

In the third week of June, Chris Murley traveled to Pompano Beach, Florida, to finish his certification to dive using Trimix gases. If all went well, he hoped to earn the certification's "C card" in Florida and put his name on one of the *Seeker*'s summer charters to the *Andrea Doria*. Dan had announced that anyone who dived the *Doria* off the decks of the *Seeker* would need to be certified in the use of Trimix.

In preparation for the hoped-for trip on the *Seeker*, Chris had filled out the "Diver Data Sheet" that Dan required. He noted that he regularly took medicine for hypertension. Joe Jackson, Chris's instructor at the Cincinnati Diving Center, also had a 1997 letter on file from a physician, Dr. Freidoon Ghazi. The doctor's note cleared Murley for scuba, alluding to Chris's "history of hypertension, which has been under control for several years" and that "from a cardiac standpoint," the six-foot-eight and 320-pound Chris "is allowed to participate in scuba diving." That spring, however, Chris also diagnosed with diabetes, according to Mary Beth Byrne. He did not include this fact on any of the release forms he signed in May 1999, either with Joe Jackson or with Dan.

Even as Chris worked toward his Trimix certification, Dan made routine exceptions to this requirement for the divers on the *Seeker*. It was difficult to see why, other than for public relations reasons, Dan called the Trimix requirement a policy. It was more like a preference, a druther. The first exceptions were made for some of Dan's crew members. People such as Gary Gentile had dived the *Andrea Doria* for years using regular air in their tanks and they could continue to do so, without becoming certified in Trimix. That seemed fair.

Dan also made exceptions for Trimix students. As odd as it seemed to some inside and outside the diving community, Dan saw no problem with some people using the Mount Everest of scuba diving for "checkout" dives to complete their training in, among other things, the safe use of Trimix. There was a caveat: An instructor had to be along, someone Dan trusted. For example, Joe Jackson, Chris Murley's instructor.

Judging from the *Seeker*'s charter schedule in the summer of 1999, Dan had put the previous summer behind him. As much as he drew his crew from the elite of the Northeast's wreck divers, he accepted customers from everywhere, and from everywhere they came with enthusiam. The red vinyl bunks were always filled with cave divers from Florida and lawyers from Washington and scuba shop instructors from across the country. If a minor regional figure such as Nick Caruso had challenged Dan, and perhaps with good reason, it didn't much matter to the larger scuba world. Dan had also spoken during the off season at DEMA, an annual trade show held that year in New Orleans. There, he had laid out the scenario he felt was true for each of the 1998 deaths. The audience was composed largely of his peers—charter captains, scuba instructors, manufacturers' reps. While Dan could not prevent others from criticizing him, or even filing lawsuits, he had done his best to make sure his spin was in circulation among people who naturally helped prospective customers shape their views.

By summer, it was hard to tell whether anything had changed. The *Seeker* was as busy as it ever had been—busier, even. Eleven different groups of divers had signed on with Dan to go the *Andrea Doria*.

A month before his scheduled trip to the *Doria*, Chris Murley completed three dives in Florida. In sharp contrast to the environment he would contend with at the *Andrea Doria*, the conditions in Florida were mild. On one of the wrecks, the water temperature reached eighty-one degrees; on another, seventy-seven. The divers could see fifty feet in any direction, minimum. At the *Doria*, where the water at the wreck was in the midforties, a dive with fifty-foot visibility was rare.

Chris used Trimix on all three of the Florida dives. On June 18, according to his diving log, he dived to 172 feet and spent one hour and nineteen minutes in the water as he explored the ruins of the *Hydroatlantic*, a 320-foot freighter that had sunk under tow in 1987. The next day, he dropped to 196 feet and stayed one hour and twenty-two minutes as he poked around the wreck of the *Lowrance*. The *Lowrance* was a 420-foot freighter sunk as an artificial reef, and the top of its superstructure, at 158 feet deep, was comparable to the depth of the highest point on the *Andrea Doria*. On June 20, on a seventy-nine-minute dive, he went to 259 feet at the wreck of the 170-foot freighter *RB Johnson*.

The dives and the hours of exposure outdoors appeared to exhaust Chris. He napped between dives. When the other men went to dinner together, he slept in his hotel room. Chris completed the dives, but he struggled. There were swells and current in Florida, even if the waters were warm. He fumbled a bit with the equipment he shouldered, and he was slow to change regulators at the correct times. Jackson had Chris and the other students under his instruction hover together deep in the water and inflate a lift bag, but Chris had trouble maintaining the right buoyancy. He kicked his fins to stay in place and tangled the men's lines together. As a Trimix diver, Jackson told others, Chris needed fine-tuning.

Chris needed Jackson's assent to make one of the *Doria* trips, and Jackson bluntly told him he needed to work harder. While Jackson was concerned about Chris's skills in the water, he told others he was equally disturbed by the man's attitude. Chris stated plainly that he intended to penetrate the wreck of the *Andrea Doria* as soon as possible. When Jackson told him that he wasn't at all certain that he would allow Chris to go into the wreck, Chris said fine, he'd go on someone else's charter.

Under the standards of Technical Diving International, the diving agency whose courses Jackson oversaw at the Cincinnati Diving Center, the instructor had to vouch for the candidate's sound judgment on dive planning and execution. As with many diving standards set by these agencies, this was a highly elastic benchmark. Still, Jackson didn't think Chris had met the test. Chris's expressed intention of unbolting toilets and faucets deep within a massive shipwreck did not represent sound judgment, to say the least. It was endearing in a way, this big talk from the big man, but it was also ridiculous. While Chris had made many dives in the cold dark water of Gilboa Quarry, he had no idea of the conditions at the *Doria*. In divers' parlance, Chris was "overaggressive." So Jackson withheld Chris's Trimix C card. In good conscience, he felt, there was nothing else for him to do.

Closer to home a week later, the ever-determined Chris

accompanied Jackson on a body-recovery mission at Lake Herrington, in Kentucky. A thirty-nine-year-old man named Jesse Ray Harness had drowned more than a month earlier. Chris was part of a team of divers who volunteered to find Harness's body. The lake is more than 250 feet deep in places, and the state of Kentucky had shut down the recovery operations two weeks earlier, citing the dangers of the lake's underwater debris, visibility of less than ten feet, and cold water temperatures (it was in the forties below a hundred feet). The other divers used Trimix that day and they all dived to two hundred feet in the unsuccessful effort to find Harness. In his two dives that day, Chris used regular air and dived to only ninety-eight feet, then sixty-nine feet. According to the log he filled out that afternoon, he was in the water thirty-four minutes for the first dive and twenty-nine minutes for the second, shallower dive. Chris continued to struggle, but he was hanging tough, and he was not giving up.

A week later, Joe Jackson had good news for Chris Murley: He had decided Chris could give the *Andrea Doria* a try. He would make checkout dives for his Trimix certification on the famed wreck. But Jackson set firm conditions. He wanted Chris's agreement to make the dives only with him and to make no penetration of the wreck; this would only be a swim along the outside. Bringing back a toilet was out of the question.

The trip was scheduled for July 16—two weeks off, and Chris was thrilled. Mary Beth Byrne, who had trained as a diver with Chris (though not to his level), was also excited, and Chris secretly decided that the two of them would be married on the *Seeker* by Captain Dan Crowell, if he was willing. It was to be a sparkling and happy weekend: Chris would marry Mary Beth, and he would explore the wreck of the *Andrea Doria*. He had agreed to Jackson's conditions, but still, deep down, he wanted to get that toilet.

Chris drove out to the quarry at Gilboa in the next two weeks and made four more dives—to depths of 62 feet, 118 feet, 112 feet, and 48 feet. The last dive was his eighty sixth since he'd first walked into Joe Jackson's shop about seventeen months earlier. Of these dives, Chris had made thirty-three of them at Gilboa.

On one of the afternoons there, as Chris was standing on the beach, shifting his scuba equipment around on his back, tweaking the straps here and there, all in all not looking especially comfortable, a familiar-looking figure approached. It was Joel Silverstein.

Silverstein was training some other divers at the quarry. A bustling scuba-training site in the middle of nowhere, Gilboa attracted divers from southern Ohio and northern Kentucky, all of them making the final highway turn onto Old State Road 224 where a giant fiberglass cow marked the way. Silverstein, while an accomplished open-ocean diver, nevertheless was impressed by Gilboa. The limestone-mining operation had shut down in 1941, and now the pit was covered by fourteen acres of surface water. In places, the quarry dropped to 140 feet. Springs fed the pool with forty-five-degree water, and a layer of sulfur in the water at sixty feet blocked out most ambient light. Even with these challenging attributes, however, Gilboa lacked qualities that made it, in isolation, a sufficient place for prospective deep wreck divers. "It's a good place for people to do training," Silverstein said. "But when you don't dive in an ocean, you don't have currents. You don't have a rocking boat, you don't have the fatigue from being on that boat. At a place like Gilboa, you can get a false sense of security."

Silverstein asked Chris if he remembered they had met a few months earlier at the conference in Columbus. Chris said yes and announced to Silverstein that he definitely was going to the *Andrea Doria.* "So," said Silverstein, "do you think you're ready?"

"My instructor says I am."

Again, from Silverstein's perspective, this was the wrong answer. He felt that divers preparing for the *Andrea Doria* needed to have a more confident attitude. To Silverstein, Chris's apparent passivity was almost as memorable as his imposing size. Passive technical divers were an exceptionally unusual subset of an already uncommon breed. Although Chris was not his student, Silverstein decided to lend advice. "If you don't think you're ready," he said, "you might want to pass on it."

"Naaah," Chris replied. "I have it scheduled for this year."

On July 15, Chris, Mary Beth, and another Cincinnati diver named Rick Lay left in Chris's brand-new Chevrolet Tahoe SUV for Long Island. Chris slept almost the entire drive. He seemed in a constant state of fatigue, as far as Mary Beth was concerned. Chris had asked her to come along, and while she was not enthusiastic about a ten-hour boat ride in the North Atlantic, she agreed because Chris wanted her to go. She also started to get a vague feeling that Chris would propose marriage to her.

When the SUV from Cincinnati arrived the next day in Montauk, Dan did not like what he saw. He could not help noticing that Chris, in Dan's description, was a "great big fat guy." Dan did not believe in luck. He thought of himself as a realist. But he was glad to have the horror of the previous summer behind him, and he did not feel he should push the limits of safe diving now with this giant of a man toting his gear down the docks at Star Island.

Still, he took Joe Jackson's word that Chris was a capable diver. No, he was not up to making a sophisticated penetration dive on the *Andrea Doria*, but he could make a landing on the wreck and manage a harmless swim along the Promenade Deck. And while Chris Murley was hardly in top shape, Dan also knew that scuba divers' bodies came in all forms. They did not have the physiques of competitive runners or body builders. Most were strong, some very strong, but not especially buff. In the end, safe diving had more to do with mental sharpness and strong training than with chiseled physiques. The evidence over the years bore that out.

To Jackson's chagrin, Chris that day also carried a reel of light-weight, stainless-steel cable. It was a safety line, used by divers to help guide themselves back out of wrecks. Obviously, Chris had plans to break the agreement he had made with Jackson back in Ohio; he wanted to get inside the wreck, and he hoped to use the cable to get back out. Chris tried to talk Jackson into changing his mind, but Jackson wouldn't budge.

Dan didn't like the look of the cable, either. He knew Chris had trained as a cave diver. Most cave divers used nylon safety line that they could cut in an emergency, not stainless steel. Dan didn't approve. He believed divers who were inexperienced with using the lines on wrecks could become entangled. The lines made this type of complicated diving even more "task-loading." He'd speak to Joe Jackson about this.

Dan and some of the other *Seeker* divers, also opposed to safety lines, instead advocated what was known as "progressive penetration" of wrecks such as the *Andrea Doria*—pushing farther and farther into the wrecks with each successive dive, memorizing key features every time. The idea was to become so well acquainted with the wreck that navigation in low-visibility conditions would become second nature, and that guide lines would thus be unnecessary. It was a purist approach to exploring the wrecks, and so difficult to argue against. Who would contend that divers should not know the wrecks backward and forward? But not everyone's lives were structured in such a way that allowed for the gradual approach dictated by progressive penetration. Few people made a minimum of twenty dives on the *Andrea Doria* each summer, as did Gentile, Moyer, and Dan. To some of the occasional visitors to the *Andrea Doria*, safety lines seemed prudent.

The sea conditions turned bad that night and Dan decided not to proceed to the *Doria*. Instead, he steered the *Seeker* to the safe harbor at Block Island, roughly ten miles east of Montauk. The next day, he ferried the group to the popular wreck of the *U-853*. The German submarine, the last sunk in U.S. waters during World War II, lies in 130 feet of water. Chris used Trimix and spent about an hour in the water before Dan took the boat back to Montauk on Saturday afternoon, July 17. The *Seeker* would make for the *Doria* on Monday.

Chris slept the entire rest of the day. Mary Beth Byrne says he slept all day Sunday, too. He ate little. He clearly wasn't himself. Mary Beth woke him early on Monday, so they could look around Montauk. They went to Star Island at about 6 and spent the evening aboard the *Seeker*, which left the dock at 11 that night. It was July 19. This time, the *Seeker* sailed in clear weather.

A crew of six accompanied the four customers from Cincinnati—Chris, Joe Jackson, Rick Lay, and Rick Vanover. Mary Beth Byrne went along as an observer and as someone expecting to be married when she returned. The crew was composed of the *Seeker*'s regulars; besides Dan and Jenn, Moyer and Gentile were along; also, the "two Steves," Brozyna and Nagiewicz. The Cincinnati divers had chartered the boat for three days for $925.

As the boat motored out to sea, Mary Beth Byrne and Joe Jackson talked about how Chris was acting and feeling. He was hardly eating. He was drinking water constantly. Mary Beth also recalled a discussion of Chris's recent diagnosis with diabetes. Mary Beth expressed concern that the diagnosis would affect Chris's ability to dive safely.

Jackson recalled only a general conversation about diabetes, and he says he was not told that Chris had been diagnosed with the disorder. He told Mary Beth that diabetes affected different people in different ways. Jackson could see however, that Chris was suffering from seasickness as the *Seeker* powered over the ocean swells. Chris admitted as much. He had been seasick with Jackson on boats before. But Jackson probed further. He was concerned that something more serious could be bothering his student. All this sleep, the huge intake of water—was it diabetes? he asked. Chris said no to all of it.

Jenn Samulski, as usual, oversaw the recording of the divers' planned air mixes and dive plans. Chris told her that his two main tanks, the large ones he would use as he swam around the wreck, would be filled with a blend of 18 percent oxygen, 15 percent helium, and the rest nitrogen. He planned a ninety-seven-minute dive that morning, including twenty-five minutes down on the wreck itself.

None of Chris's previous eighty-six dives had ever lasted ninety-seven minutes.

He and Joe Jackson entered the water together at 10:49 A.M. Chris safely made his way to the anchor line and began the descent. At fifty feet, though, he stopped. He signaled to Jackson that he was having trouble breathing the mix from the tanks. He decided to abort the dive. He couldn't pull himself aboard with all the gear on, so he took off some of the tanks in the water and handed them up. Joe Jackson, who had ascended with his student and made sure Chris got aboard the boat, then turned back down and made his dive on the *Doria*.

Up on the deck of the *Seeker*, Chris sat down wearily on the dressing table. He quietly told Mary Beth that his vision was obscured by a blue haze. Then he took a nap, ate some food, and reported that the haze was gone. As darkness fell, and the ocean turned from blue to black, Chris said he felt much better. Informed later of Chris's blue haze, Jackson was perplexed. He had never heard of such a reaction. He asked the other divers. They hadn't, either.

The next morning, Chris and Jackson splashed into the water at 8:44 A.M., and this time things went smoothly for Chris. He and Jackson had planned to bottom out their dive at 210 feet and stay down there for twenty-five minutes, but they stopped at 198 feet and remained there for only twenty-one minutes. Nevertheless, Chris made the classic first-timer *Doria* dive. He swam along the Promenade Deck, where divers crept along above the skeletal symmetry of the long line of window frames. Jackson then skirted across the hull, patchy with barnacles, and dropped into Gimbel's Hole. He positioned himself in front of the passageways that led to the wreck's interior and signaled for Chris to follow.

Jackson said Chris lowered himself about three feet into the opening. Technically, the maneuver might not count as a wreck penetration. Chris did not go far enough into the hole for him to be in an overhead environment. Yet plunging into Gimbel's Hole was not the same as swimming outside, which is what Jackson and Chris had agreed to. As was his custom, Dan had also urged all the divers new to the *Doria* to remain outside the wreck and to be content with a swim outside the hulk, but such advice was routinely ignored.

Seventeen months from the first time he first strapped on a scuba tank, Chris had dived on the wreck of the *Andrea Doria,* and a few would say he even penetrated the ship. Certainly, he had accomplished the feat with a paid guide almost holding his hand—Joe Jackson—but he made it safely back to the boat. Chris's success argued for the variability among divers that people such as Dan frequently pointed out. Yes, he would say, it made sense to have everyone who dived the *Andrea Doria* be certified for Trimix, even if just to be exposed to the advanced techniques, even if the diver did not plan to use Trimix. But even divers who were studying for the certification could make a *Doria* dive safely. Chris Murley, the big fat guy Dan had quietly derided, had provided the proof.

Before the men began their decompression, Jackson wrote "Good Dive" on the underwater slate they had carried down to the wreck with them. When he got back on the *Seeker,* Chris took the slate and asked Mary Beth to take a photograph of him holding it. Later, in sketchy penmanship no doubt caused by the movement of the *Seeker* on the ocean, Chris noted the dive in the "Comments" section of his dive log: "Crossed Promenade Deck + into Gimbel's Hole—Per Joe Dive Went Well."

Jackson planned an afternoon dive for all four of the divers from Cincinnati—himself, Chris, and veteran divers Rick Vanover and Rick Lay. Jackson told Chris to remain outside the ship. No poking around Gimbel's Hole this time. Chris was irritated. Here he had come all this distance, and had shown he could do the dive, and he had to wait outside the wreck.

His irritation whipped into anger. Chris offered Jackson a thousand dollars on the spot to take him inside the wreck. Jackson said no. Chris explained that he wanted the toilet and sink fixtures. He thought of the plans for a *Doria*-themed room for the home he and Mary Beth shared. He pulled out the reel of stainless-steel safety line. Wouldn't the line make a deep penetration OK?

Jackson told him no again.

To the other divers, Chris seemed either delusional or shockingly uninformed. It seemed he had no idea of the absurdity of the notion that someone such as himself, who seventeen months earlier had not even strapped on a single can of compressed air, should be allowed to penetrate the wreck of the *Andrea Doria* as deeply as people such as Gary Gentile. Even in the fast and loose subculture of Northeast wreck diving, this was dangerously risky.

Jackson told Chris he wouldn't be diving if he didn't abide by the agreed-upon plan. There would be no compromise. This had the effect of shutting Chris up. He agreed.

Dan also made a late-afternoon dive that day. He entered the water a few minutes before 5.

Chris and Jackson now sat on the *Seeker*'s dressing table, making final preparations. It was a spectacular afternoon on top of the ocean: Temperatures were in the seventies, visibility measured at least ten miles, and a mild wind from the north provided a cooling breeze to the divers in their stifling neoprene suits. Mary Beth tucked Chris's hoses away for him and tugged on straps that held the decompression bottles in their places. Chris decided to make one more run at Jackson, and he again offered his instructor a thousand dollars to take him inside the *Andrea Doria*. Jackson glared at him.

Chris walked over and knelt at the cutout along the *Seeker*'s starboard rail. Then, at 5:12 P.M., he dropped into the water. He quickly surfaced, looked for Mary Beth, and held up an OK sign. She took a picture. In a few seconds, after Chris had gotten out of the way, Jackson rolled into the ocean.

Then Chris began pulling himself along what the divers called a geri line—a rope that ran along the length of the boat, descended below the water's surface, and knotted into the anchor line. It eased the diver's brief trip to the anchor line.

Submerged just below the surface, Chris inched along the geri line. He was horizontal in the water, about fifteen feet ahead of Jackson, who could see Chris's fins paddling the water.

Jackson glanced down at his tanks, and when he looked back up Chris had stopped.

Now Chris was vertical in the water. Jackson saw him from only the chest down.

"Help me!" Chris cried.

Jackson hurried as best he could to get to Chris.

"Help me!" Chris repeated.

Moyer, who had been in the *Seeker's* cockpit, recording the divers' entry times, sprinted down the *Seeker's* stairs. He and diver Steve Nagiewicz met up and hustled to the bow.

They saw that Jackson had made it to Chris's side. The two men were under the *Seeker's* long bowsprit. Neither Chris's buoyancy-compensator vest nor his suit was inflated. To Nagiewicz, it looked like the 320-pound Chris was having difficulty staying afloat.

"I'm drowning," Chris cried. "Help me."

Nagiewicz jumped into the water. He and Jackson tried to get Chris to accept a regulator and breathe and relax, but Chris wouldn't cooperate. He flailed his arms. "Help me," he cried, again and again.

Jenn and Moyer lowered a line to Chris and, with what entailed a tremendous physical strain, he attempted to pull himself out of the water. He was in a full-blown panic. He continued to fight off Nagiewicz and Jackson. Nagiewicz pushed the inflation button on Chris's vest and on his dry suit, and that helped. Chris lifted in the water a bit and he calmed down. Gary Gentile had the line from the boat now.

"I'll tow you," he called.

Chris stopped flailing. He lay on his back, with his main air tanks in Jackon's face; Nagiewicz had his legs. Gentile towed them along the length of the boat, from the bow toward the stern.

Then, halfway back, Chris stopped talking. He stopped moving.

It was if he had suffered a heart attack. That's what it looked like to the others. Chris just slumped.

"It doesn't look like he's breathing," Jenn Samulski called from on deck.

Now Steve Brozyna, another crew member, splashed in. He began to administer mouth-to-mouth resuscitation on Chris. Then John Moyer handed a knife down from on deck and Brozyna used it to begin sawing away at Chris's equipment straps. Nagiewicz and Jackson began handing the gear up to Vanover and others on board. Rick Lay jumped in. He held Chris's head out of the water as Brozyna continued the rescue breathing.

Jenn jotted notes as the men struggled with Chris. At 5:19, seven minutes after Chris had splashed in, the crew members had him at the back of the boat. At first they all tried to bundle Chris up the ladder, but that proved impossible

They tried a rope under his arms and tried to lift him. Still, no go. He was way too big a man. So they floated him all the way around the *Seeker*'s stern to the portside, where the boat had a block and tackle, and they used that to slowly hoist him aboard.

It was 5:26. Fourteen minutes had passed since Chris had entered the water.

Moyer had called the Coast Guard, and once they got Chris on the boat, they lifted him to the dressing table, where they continue to administer CPR for another hour. Gary Gentile helped with chest compressions but, alone among those aboard, he decided to make his scheduled afternoon dive. He entered the water at 5:39.

When Gentile returned, at 6:35 P.M., a Coast Guard helicopter once again had lumbered out from Cape Cod, hovered above the *Seeker,* and dropped down a rescue swimmer. The swimmer helped secure Chris Murley onto a litter, and they took Chris aboard the helicopter. He was pronounced dead on arrival in a Cape Cod hospital.

Not long after the helicopter had roared toward the horizon, Joe Jackson asked a stunned Mary Beth Byrne how many dives Chris had made, total. Eighty-nine, she said, off by a couple of dives.

Then why, Joe asked, would Chris would have said he had completed more dives? Mary Beth was not sure what Jackson meant by the question, except that Jackson had given Chris material for his "Advanced Trimix Diver Course" that listed as a prerequisite a "minimum of 100 logged dives or equivalent at the discretion of the instructor."

She told Jackson he could always look at Chris's official PADI Diver's Log and Training Record. Jackson himself had signed pages in this log many times, to indicate that Chris had passed one test or another. Jackson had taken Chris through virtually all his diving courses.

Dan quaked with anger when he came out of the water and learned what had happened. He had sensed that Chris wasn't fit to dive. He knew it. It seemed obvious. But he had trusted Joe Jackson, with whom he had worked for several years. Absent enforceable, straightforward standards, and, apparently, his own willingness to set firm rules and stick to them, this was Dan's world: He relied on people vouching for each other, and he made exceptions to the rules when it suited him. Soon he, Jackson, and

Mary Beth were discussing Chris's medical history. There was the hypertension. Mary Beth mentioned the diabetes diagnosis. She also said Chris's parents had both had heart problems.

Just as news of Vince Napoliello's heart problems had, in a sick sense, relieved Dan, so did this news. As far as Dan was concerned, this fatality hardly counted as a diving death. Chris wasn't diving. He was on the surface. A heart attack waiting to happen. Wasn't it obvious? Another freak accident. Not so much bad luck, but yet another consequence of taking the highest numbers of divers to the *Doria*. It was cruel mathematics.

With Mary Beth aboard—she let news of the wedding plan slip—there was no question about remaining at the dive site. They had to pull anchor. The *Seeker* never stayed after a diver death. They were there, after all, for fun, and the accidents deflated everyone's high spirits. At least for a few days, the fun was gone. In a way also, Mary Beth was a source of discomfort if only because she was so clearly devastated. She was not part of this group; she had been encouraged to go inside the *Seeker*'s cabin as the crew worked to get her fiancée back aboard, and she had not been asked to provide a statement to the Coast Guard, as had everyone else on the boat.

By 7, the dive boat was pointed back to Montauk. The early evening remained clear and warm but the northern breeze had shifted since the morning, so now the *Seeker* was turned against the wind.

The staff at the Massachusetts Office of the Chief Medical Examiner, in Pocasset, waited a day before conducting the autopsy on Chris. Dr. George Kury listed the cause of death as drowning. Other "significant conditions," he found, were an enlarged heart and Chris's obesity.

In the next few days, the findings of the autopsy were relayed to Mary Beth and Jackson, then eventually to Dan. Sadly, Dan believed, his concerns about Chris's being a "great big fat guy" had been confirmed.

Joe Jackson drove Mary Beth back to Cincinnati. She couldn't bring herself to call Chris's father and tell him what had happened, so Jackson did it for her. She wasn't comfortable in either Chris's parents' home or even her own parents' house, so she found herself going to the Cincinnati Diving Center almost every day. She had been there countless times with Chris. This was part of her social community. For the most part, Jackson was sympathetic. He helped her find a counseling program for her younger son, who was upset at the death of Chris. That meant a lot to her.

Mary Beth felt herself sinking into depression. After five divorces between them, she and Chris had found each other. She believed she had found love and stability and someone to grow old with. Now he was lost, and so was she. Eventually, though, anger started to rise in her. She couldn't help feeling that Chris never should have been aboard the *Seeker*. She had been around enough divers to know that Chris seemed out of his league on the famous charter boat. She began to question why the *Seeker* had allowed Chris in the water after the blue-haze dive. She still had not found out what, if any, physical problem the blue haze could have signaled, but now it seemed to her the safest thing to do that day would have been to tell Chris to pack up his gear and sit out the dives.

Several weeks after Chris's death, Mary Beth contacted Joe Jackson and asked if she could have Chris's C card for Trimix. Her reasons were unclear but certainly sentimental. She and Chris were to have been married on the boat on the day he died. She knew it wasn't logical. For some reason, getting Chris's C card would have been a comfort to her.

Jackson refused. He didn't see the value in giving the card to Mary Beth. She had not earned the certification. Under the rules, he was supposed to give the card to the person who had done all the training that was required.

Chris, Jackson explained, had not completed the necessary dives.

Ten

CHARLIE

A week after the death of Chris Murley, the *Seeker* was back on top of the *Andrea Doria* wreck site. Besides Dan and Jenn Samulski, the crew once again included Gary Gentile and Steve Nagiewicz. Also on the crew was Pete Wohlleben, a plumbing contractor who did a lot of work on the *Seeker* engines, and Charlie McGurr.

Charlie's trip was a birthday present to himself. He turned fifty-two on July 27, four days after he drove north to New York, then east across Long Island and to Montauk. Like Dan and Jenn, he lived in Brick, and he and Dan had become good friends in the previous few years. He worked at Brick Auto Body, and he and his wife, Kathy, ran the 18th Avenue Beach House, a sports bar in South Belmar. He had been diving for six years, and he relished bringing up clams and mussels to serve at the bar.

At Brick Auto Body, McGurr was the one who took on most of what they called the "hard hits," the cars most heavily damaged. Even if other guys took the jobs, Charlie was asked his opinion. Charlie was just the sort of guy Dan liked to be around. He didn't sit around and watch TV. He wasn't a Manhattan office worker who had taken up extreme sports in his thirties. Charlie had long competed in skydiving competitions. He was a former Army Green Beret, but you would never know it. He didn't tell many war stories.

Charlie had dived the *Andrea Doria* the previous summer and had even come away with a plate that said ITALIA on it. He told people the plate was his most cherished possession. Despite that dive, however, Charlie had not been diving with much regularity. He did not have the Trimix certification when he'd dived on the wreck the previous summer; he was one of the *Seeker* family, and had been one of Dan's exceptions to the rules. He and Kathy had been running hard to make the bar successful, and he still had the job at the auto body shop. He had earned his last C card, for another kind of mixed-gas diving, in 1997. Dan had been the instructor, holding the classes in a den behind his garage.

The Friday night before the trip, Charlie stopped by the bar, packed a couple of coolers full of ice for the trip, kissed Kathy good-bye, and hit the road for Montauk.

That summer, Dan wanted Charlie to get the Trimix certification before he went to the *Andrea Doria* for his birthday. With Gary Gentile's help, Dan helped Charlie log the necessary dives, and Charlie got the C card on July 2.

The morning of July 27, before 9 A.M., he and Gentile made the tie-in dives, when the *Seeker* hooked into the wreck. Right away they noticed that the current was strong. When they surfaced, they could hear it sizzling as it eddied around the anchor line where it went into the water.

Eight customers were aboard for the charter, and Dan spoke to them all about the current. The divers needed to be ready for the water's speed. It would affect them the most when they prepared to swim from the boat to the anchor line and when they began to work their way down the anchor line. People needed to keep in mind that every action would require more physical effort. That, in turn, could mean they would inhale more from their tanks. It was a day to keep a close eye on the pressure gauges.

Divers become acutely aware of a strong ocean current during their decompression stops: Hanging on to the anchor line with a five-mile-an-hour current can be like trying to stand still in ocean surf. The danger is that divers blown off the anchor line could ascend too rapidly and be carried away, beyond help. Under just such circumstances, divers' bodies have been found miles from their boats.

To make sure they did not separate from the anchor line, many divers attached themselves to it with short pieces of rope. Clipped in this way, they were underwater kites, popped off the line a few feet, but safely tethered.

The night of July 27, Charlie spent some time patching his dry suit where a pinhole leak had developed. The others aboard presented him with a cupcake blazing with candles and serenaded him with "Happy Birthday."

On the morning of the twenty-eighth, Charlie and fellow crew member Wohlleben prepared to escort *Seeker* customer Darryl Johnson down to the wreck. They planned to go to 210 feet on the dive. Johnson, Wohlleben and Charlie splashed into the water at 8:59, 9:00, and 9:01 respectively, and soon they were moving down the anchor line like beads of dew sliding down a spider's thread. Wohlleben led, followed by Johnson, and Charlie brought up the rear.

At forty feet down, they began to encounter other divers who had gone into the water earlier, but who were now on their way back up. They were hanging on the line, pausing at prescribed intervals for their decompression stops. First they came upon Alston Trent and Jackie Smith. Wary of the current, Wohlleben and Johnson picked their way over first Trent then Smith, taking care to never lose contact with the anchor line.

Charlie decided to pass Trent and Smith at the same time. He had passed Trent and was moving past Smith when, as the two decompressing divers watched, he lost his grip.

His black-gloved hand stretched for the anchor line throbbing in the current.

But in a breath he was several feet away from the line, as if someone had hog-tied his ankles and yanked hard.

Charlie pumped his fins furiously.

His opened hand slowly moved toward the anchor line.

More hard swimming.

A few more seconds. Fins snapping up and down. Then, he had the line. He hugged it hard. He hung there for a few breaths.

Then he was on his way. He intended to catch up with Wohlleben. He wasn't sure he wanted to continue the dive. At about seventy feet down, his form disappeared from Smith's view. Charlie caught up with his two dive buddies, but at about 150 feet down—20 feet or so above the reef-like hull of the *Andrea Doria*—he signaled to Wohlleben.

He raised a thumb in the air. He was aborting his dive and going back up. Then, the OK sign. He was fine.

That morning, visibility on the *Doria* was superb—about eighty feet. Wohlleben had no problem seeing Charlie's hand motions. He figured Charlie was tired. He and Johnson proceeded with their dive.

Charlie had not indicated that anything was wrong, so no

reason existed for Wohlleben to break off his dive to see if he could assist. Charlie had a reputation for caution underwater. Even if he had signaled he had a problem, no particular expectation held that another diver would come to his aid. It depended completely on the circumstances of the moment. In Charlie's case, other *Seeker* divers had seen him previously abort dives. It was the smart thing to do if you were not sure. Maybe the dry suit leak had reopened. The prudent approach was to cut the dive short, surface, try again later.

After his exploration of the shipwreck, Darryl Johnson began his decompression stops. Although Charlie would have been twenty minutes ahead of him, and visibility on the line was only about thirty feet—murkier than on the wreck—he thought he might see Charlie hanging on the line above him, on his way back up. He never did. As soon as he got back on the *Seeker*, at 10:18, he asked about Charlie.

No on else had seen him, either.

Pete Wohlleben was also surprised that he had not seen Charlie as he ascended on his decompression. He asked about it as soon as he surfaced, at 10:25.

Dan immediately became concerned. At Dan's request, Wohlleben went back down the anchor line to do a head count. No Charlie. Charlie was due out of the water at just past 10:30, so Dan had no choice but to begin an intensive search for his friend. Dan put Wohlleben and Steve Nagiewicz in the *Seeker's* inflatable Zodiac to look for Charlie on the surface. They took the little boat as far as two miles downcurrent from the *Seeker*. A customer, Joe King, climbed to the pilothouse and scanned the waters with binoculars. Dan called the Coast Guard at 10:55.

Within minutes, a search helicopter lifted off from the air station on Cape Cod, forty-five miles to the north.

Diver Michael Carpenter surfaced just past 11, and Dan had many questions about what he had seen. But Carpenter explained that he had felt winded when he hit the *Doria's* hull and had begun an immediate ascent. He never poked around the ship. He hadn't seen a thing.

The Coast Guard at Woods Hole, Massachusetts, decided now to issue an "Urgent Marine Information Broadcast." It crackled over the *Seeker's* marine-band radio.

"The Coast Guard received a report of an overdue diver in Position 40-29.39 North, 069-51.49 West at the site of the sunken vessel *Andrea Doria*. Mariners are requested to keep a sharp lookout."

With Charlie now ninety minutes overdue, some on the *Seeker* began to accept what to them seemed unavoidable. For a while, with denial the best alternative to the sad reality, some of the divers clung to the hope that Charlie was struggling through a "floating decompression," in which divers ascend by increments without the use of an anchor line. It took a good diver to pull that off. Charlie McGurr was not deeply experienced in these particular waters, but he seemed like the kind of man who could bull through that situation, even with the weather deteriorating at midday. For an hour or so, hope partially eclipsed despair.

Carpenter's dive buddy, Michael Kane, emerged from the water at just past noon. After Carpenter had aborted his dive, Kane had stayed. He had entered the ship at Gimbel's Hole and, outside the hull, had swum to depths of 230 feet. He had seen much of the wreck. Quickly debriefed, he gave the answer no one wanted. He said he had not seen Charlie.

By 12:30, the Coast Guard helicopter was above the *Seeker*, looking for Charlie. Ten minutes later, Dan entered the water with one of the charter's customers. J. T. Barker was a dive instructor from Portsmouth, Virginia (he called himself "Captain J. T." there), and Dan decided to take him to a part of the wreck site Barker had never seen. They would check the debris field. This was the sprawling area next to the ship where the *Doria*'s funnel had thudded into the sand forty-three years earlier, and where sawed-off stanchions and cargo booms held fishing nets, which cascaded like bridal veils from above. The debris field is 230 feet down, and Barker labored to keep up with Dan, who'd combed this area dozens of times and had a sense of where a body might fall and become wedged.

Visibility had worsened since divers were in the water earlier. At 230 feet, Dan and Barker could see 10 feet in front of them. They were like catfish, pecking along the bottom.

They saw nothing, however, and began to ascend, past the hanging nets, toward the ship's port hull, into which the *Seeker* was anchored.

Like climbers reaching the top of a cliff from below, they reached the hull and began moving across. They were within ten feet of Gimbel's Hole when Dan saw him. He waved Barker over. Charlie's face was pressed into the rotting sheets of steel that had once supported the Promenade Deck. He was motionless, and he did not respond. The dive light attached to his dry suit continued to emit a beam, wan in the dwindling visibility now. Plankton gathered at the illumination, spinning in the light.

Charlie was wedged somehow in the wreck. His regulator was out of his mouth. Dan dropped down to Charlie's left and Barker to his right and they spent a few moments looking at him. Charlie was so close to Gimbel's Hole, where other divers had been. Why hadn't anyone seen him? The answer had a few parts to it. Charlie had come to rest at a spot that placed him behind divers who would have exited Gimbel's Hole and proceeded to the *Seeker's* anchor line. Divers often created their own silt clouds as they moved around on the wreck. The silt created small, diver-sized zones of poor visibility even on a day when the overall visibility was good. Finally, they weren't looking for him.

Dan and Barker saw that Charlie's decompression stage bottles had not been deployed, which suggested that Charlie, for some reason, had fallen down from somewhere in the water above to this spot. His manifold valve, which allowed breathing gases to be drawn down from both tanks, was in the correct ON position. Dan pushed a button on Charlie's buoyancy compensator, in an effort to get some lift on Charlie. The device's inflatable wings filled with air, but Charlie's body didn't budge.

Then they saw that his feet were stuck under something on the wreck, and they freed him. Barker then unclipped Charlie's twenty-eight-pound weight belt and Charlie's body began to drift upward. As they watched, he continued to rise until after about twenty feet he ascended into the blackness, the flame of his dive light erased by the gloom.

Charlie hit the surface close to the *Seeker*. Kane, Carpenter, and Trent jumped into the water and towed him closer to the boat. Kane saw that Charlie's lips were blue. Someone else felt for a pulse and there was none, so this time no one performed

CPR. The Coast Guard had already told Dan's crew that it would only take Charlie back on the rescue helicopter if he was alive. So the helicopter was waved off, just before 2 P.M.

Coast Guard authorities in Boston typed a press release about their involvement in the case. It noted that Charlie was the fifth diver in two summers to be lost at the wreck site. The public affairs staff in Boston faxed the statement to dozens of newspapers in the Northeast. It was the first time the agency had mentioned that a death—Chris Murley's—had taken place a week earlier.

An hour later, with Charlie's rigid body aboard, the *Seeker* made for Montauk. The voyage was bouncy. Swells had built to three feet, and seawater scribbled the cabin windows. The divers were quiet. Dan said little; this time, he knew the widow. He would tell people Charlie had been family, and it was easy to understand why. He was part of the little community from which the *Seeker* drew its crew and many of its customers, one of the divers who lived in the string of small towns squeezed between the Garden State Parkway and the Jersey shore. Charlie had been his diving student, munching on the Dunkin' Donuts laid out on the bar in the den.

The *Seeker* entered Montauk Inlet about 11 that night. The crew stopped at the Coast Guard station on Star Island, handed over Charlie's body, then motored over to the Star Island Yacht Club. At least one newspaper photographer snapped photographs as the men unloaded their gear. The tanks clinked together and thunked on the timbers of the dock. The men wore old gym shorts and dirty T-shirts; their faces had two or three days' growth.

Later, Dan and the crew ended up over at the Liar's Saloon. It's a cheap small place where Montauk's commercial fishermen and marina workers go late at night. Tourists favor the big restaurants farther out on Westlake Road, places that bought lobster traps and buoys from fishermen's supply stores and tacked them up to their walls for decoration. The effect was supposed to be the way it was in Montauk, thirty years back and more, when men from Queens and Brooklyn would take the "Fishermen's Special" train to the party boats lined up like feeding cattle at the piers of nearby Fort Pond Bay.

The Liar's Saloon had a simpler marketing strategy: DRAFT BEER $1, said the red-lettered sign out by the road. The men from the *Seeker* crunched across the gravel lot and past the *Ocean Spirit,* a lobster boat under repair.

Inside, for hours, they hoisted draft beers, $1, and toasted their dead friend Charlie. They sang along with some of the Jimmy Buffett songs on the jukebox. They played foosball. It was amusing to play foosball when you had drunk several draft beers. The foosball scores were low. There had been a death in the family.

Dan drank more that night than he had in ten years.

Eleven

In the early-August days after Charlie McGurr died, the cooling winds moved offshore from Long Island, and Montauk festered under a gluey gauze of oppressive humidity. It was as if somehow the sky had moved closer to the ground. At the end of one of the docks at the Star Island Yacht Club, Dan held court with a few reporters. He wanted nothing more than to take the boat back over to Manasquan Inlet, and home, but he had more charters booked for the *Andrea Doria*. He remained stunned by Charlie's death. But he already had begun to accept the accident as typical of recreational diving; it was. anomalous, rare. Dan answered many questions with a trademark gesture: He would run one hand from front to back across his hair, squint his eyes at his questioner, then speak. He was weary. Reporters did not resist asking the most obvious and broad question: How could he account for the five deaths over the two summer seasons?

To Dan, the question was embedded with a faulty premise. These deaths were not about the *Andrea Doria*. The wreck, he maintained, possessed no deadly magic, much less the "curse" other divers had proposed in newspaper articles during the summer. He reminded people that the vast majority of dives at the *Doria*—hundreds of dives—were made safely.

As far as Dan was concerned, one of the five deaths had involved apparently bad judgment (Craig Sicola's) while the other four had been triggered by catastrophic medical emergencies. Who knew that Vince Napoliello had a heart condition? Dan asked.

Even Vince possibly did not know because he never mentioned it on his diver-release forms, Dan explained. Four of the dead men were certified for Trimix diving and the fifth (Chris Murley) was diving with an experienced instructor, a man who had once trained divers for the Marine Corps and Navy. He insisted that each fatal dive be evaluated individually. "It's a tragic, horrible coincidence—what's gone on in the last year or fourteen months," he said. "But it's not a problem in diving, or anything like that. The way I look at it, if there were five fatalities in a bowling alley, it would be a big story. Even if they were all from heart attacks."

Jenn Samulksi echoed her partner's flinty view. "When your number's up, it's up," she said. "I'd prefer it not be on my boat, but we can't stop living because of this. Anybody's who's at the level to dive the *Doria* knows the risks involved. For most of them, it's what they enjoy doing and they are going to do it, no matter who takes them out."

Steve Bielenda also had a few things to say. Of course, he would not play the role of cheerleader for Dan Crowell. As are many self-promoters, Bielenda was a lightning rod for criticism. He was a dinosaur, some divers said. They made fun of his silver ponytail, and scoffed at his tough-guy bluster. Yet he also was accorded a measure of respect because he had devoted his life to the thrill of Northeast wreck diving and to the industry itself. "When you're putting ten or eleven trips on your schedule each summer, that means you need to fill ten or eleven trips," Bielenda said. "There just aren't enough qualified people out there to fill that many trips."

While those in the *Seeker* camp reflexively dismissed any utterance from Bielenda, they listened more openly to what their own John Moyer had to say. He was a rock-solid member of the *Seeker* camp, a crew member for the previous four years, but he articulated a far less fatalistic perspective than either Dan or Jenn. Moyer had been aboard for all the *Seeker's* deaths at the *Doria* in 1998 and 1999 except that of Charlie McGurr. Though loyal to Dan, Moyer felt that extreme wreck diving in the late 1990s was luring too many divers who weren't ready for the *Andrea Doria*. He made his opinions clear when he took the unusual action of issuing a press release.

While Moyer's statement had the ring of reinforcing his legal claim—he had the salvage rights to the *Doria*—he also took the opportunity to air his concerns about the recent cascade of fatalities. Moyer did not agree that divers under instruction should be visiting the wreck. "I don't think people realize how difficult a dive it actually is," his statement said. "Most certified technical divers lack the wreck diving expertise necessary to dive on the *Andrea Doria*. They should have made hundreds of North Atlantic wreck dives before attempting it. No amount of training can replace experience. They also need to be in top physical condition."

Other rational voices also made themselves heard. Many of these belonged to people outside the ring in which the *Seeker* and the other regional dive boats fought for primacy. They wondered aloud if the *Doria* wreck site, and the charter operations, were as safe as they should be. They accepted the risks involved in the small universe of technical diving, yet they were disturbed. These voices included even that of Peter Bennett, one of the world's prominent authorities on diving safety and a major figure in the growth of recreational diving in the 1980s and 1990s.

Bennett had one of the industry's singular careers. A native of England and veteran of the Royal Air Force, he had conducted groundbreaking research for the Royal Navy. He had measured how people's bodies reacted to underwater explosions and had concocted experimental gas mixes (including what would be known as Trimix) so submarine crews could breathe if they needed to escape while deep below the surface. He later coined the term *High Pressure Nervous Syndrome* to describe the physiological effects of deep diving—tremors, nightmares, dizziness—and advised filmmaker James Cameron on *The Abyss*, the underwater science fiction epic that is standard viewing fare on virtually every dive boat VCR.

For divers unfamiliar with Bennett's two hundred highly technical published papers, however, his renown was based on something entirely different: He founded the Divers Alert Network at Duke University in 1982. DAN, as it is known, makes physicians available around the clock to divers who have diving-related medical problems. Sometimes charter captains call DAN's headquarters in Durham, North Carolina, from their boat decks offshore, with a diver aboard writhing in pain from a hit of decompression sickness. Bennett's brainchild has 260,000 members worldwide and has served an indisputably critical need. It has referred thousands of stricken divers to treatment and also sponsors research on diving medicine and diving fatalities.

But over the years, Bennett became as much a businessman as a scientist. In a stroke of financial genius, he spun off from the not-for-profit DAN a for-profit insurance company that marketed cheap policies to divers. Bennett became chairman of the insurance corporation, which is headquartered in the Cayman Islands along with hundreds of other insurance entities seeking looser regulation. In 1999, Bennett earned a salary of $205,058 from DAN.

DAN is Bennett's crowning achievement, and the organization revolves around his personality. Its public relations department churns out releases about every one of the numerous honors he receives, and these are reprinted in DAN's colorful magazine. In 1993, DAN built a new $3.5 million headquarters in Durham, and named the four-story building for Bennett himself.

In viewing the string of deaths at the *Andrea Doria*, Bennett reminded his listeners that the number of recreational scuba deaths each year in the United States has remained roughly the same—ninety to one hundred. He also took pains to point out that Chris Murley had, after all, died on the surface. Still, he acknowledged that the numbers of injuries and fatalities specifically associated with mixed-gas diving—including dives made with the use of Trimix—were increasing. Five divers using Trimix had died in the previous two years, while in the four years before that, eight had died.

The numbers grew more sobering when they included all "technical" divers—those who had died while diving below 130 feet, or while exploring deep wrecks or submerged freshwater caves: Of the 160 diving fatalities in 1998 and 1999, 28 were "technical" divers. These twenty-eight deaths represented about 17 percent of the total number of fatalities, a percentage well above the estimated 10 percent of all divers considered to be certified for technical diving.

Such statistics certainly needed time to cure, to see if they held over several years. It was also impossible to tell what proportion of people certified for technical depths were actively diving. But the death rate for mixed-gas recreational scuba diving nevertheless approached those of the nation's deadliest occupations, commercial fishing and even logging. Because DAN purports to investigate safety issues while also promoting recreational diving, adventure travel, and accident insurance, its officers are loath to publicly criticize the industry. Bennett chose his words with care. "I'm concerned that we may have a situation every summer at the *Andrea Doria* where we have two or three deaths there," he said. "I think one of the things we can do is set up a workshop and really look at deep-diving risks and deep diving on wrecks."

Tom Doherty, who owned a dive shop in Westfield, New Jersey, up the New Jersey Turnpike from the *Seeker*'s home port in Brielle, also voiced skepticism. Doherty had been Vince Napoliello's diving instructor and he had also certified Dan a few years earlier in the use of the gas blend known as Nitrox. He was no enemy of Dan. While Doherty believed that scuba diving was a generally safe sport, he also was disturbed by what had taken place the previous two summers aboard his former student's boat. Like many others in the technical-diving community, he was asking questions: "We have to change something. Something has to give. This is impossible. This is five tragedies too many."

Lieutenant Tim Dickerson, the Coast Guard investigator, had none of Doherty's deep-diving experience. But he felt the same way as Doherty about the rash of fatalities at the *Andrea Doria*. Something had to give.

↧ ↧ ↧

A week later, the *Seeker* returned to the *Doria*.

Gentile had written what he called a eulogy for Charlie McGurr. Moyer had a wreath he planned to toss onto the water. They all stood close together in the V of the *Seeker's* bow. No such rite had taken place after the deaths of Craig Sicola, Richard Roost, Vince Napoliello, or Christopher Murley.

But Charlie McGurr was family. No one from the crew had ever died before. Dan was rarely one to describe his personal relationships in emotional terms. He and Charlie, he said, were not "buddy-buddy, or anything like that." But they were pals. Charlie had access to Dan's garage. Charlie might drive over when Dan was not there, borrow a sander, leave a joking note behind. Dan didn't think of the ceremony as only in Charlie's memory. It was for all five. This was the *Seeker's* last trip of the summer to the *Andrea Doria*. For Dan, that fact seemed to add a layer of sadness to the afternoon. Only a week before, he had been swimming along the hull of the *Doria*, searching for Charlie. There he was, facedown and dead.

Dan was barefoot and dressed in T-shirt and shorts. Jenn stood across from him, leaning back into the rail, her feet crossed at the ankles. It was one of those gentle days at sea, when the Atlantic Ocean was as calm and blue as an alpine lake. Dan read Gentile's words, which brimmed with his distinctive touches of super-serious sentimentality.

"We commend this wreath to the deep in memory of Charlie McGurr: a good man, a good friend, a great loss. That most precious commodity of human perception—that which we call life—Charlie grasped with uncommon enthusiasm. That he died doing something he liked so well is not to be shamed. We should all be so fortunate. . . ."

Moyer tossed the wreath on the water.

Then they rang the *Seeker's* bell five times, once each for the men who had breathed their last fresh air standing on its deck.

Tim Dickerson had no formal training in the investigation of scuba diving fatalities, but the U.S. government had ordered him to probe the deaths that had taken place at the wreck of the *Andrea Doria*.

Dickerson's job in New Haven was to probe vessel accidents. Usually, in the typed reports he sent to his superiors in Boston, he could pinpoint the cause of a problem. He could determine that a ferry on Long Island Sound had grounded because it had lost engine power, or that a local lobsterman had fallen overboard because he had been snared in a line snapped taut by the weight of a descending trap. When possible, Dickerson made suggestions: more frequent engine inspections for the ferry company, better crew training on the deck of the lobster boat.

With the *Seeker's* accidents, Dickerson found himself less assured. The obvious solutions to what he considered a safety problem at the *Andrea Doria* were not available to him. He could not suggest an improved maintenance schedule or make practical suggestions for the training of the *Seeker's* crew. A regulation could not be implemented to require that all divers check their isolator valves before jumping into the water. He certainly could not deny access to the sunken ship. The *Doria* was not a military property, much less a war grave, and the Coast Guard in any event could never enforce such a restriction at a site a hundred miles from shore. He sincerely believed that the fatalities could have been prevented if the divers explored the wreck in teams, but when he made public statements to this effect, they came across as naive expressions of a safety philosophy, and philosophies were not enforceable. Dickerson would have relished posing the diving accidents against some set of rules for such activities, but no rules existed. That was the problem. Tim Dickerson dealt in regulations every day of his working life, and here he was attempting to work with a community of people who had no rules.

He decided to get them all in one room. His was a bureaucrat's response, grounded in the earnest belief that somehow better communication resulted in better practices. He also felt he needed a deeper understanding of what he was investigating. Perhaps all of them together could improve what obviously was not a desirable situation.

It took a while to get the key people together. The boat rivalries flowered in all their absurdity. Once Dan learned that Steve Bielenda would be there, he did not want to participate. The meeting was also to be convened on Long Island, at the Coast Guard's office in Coram. To Dan, a Jersey wreck diver, it smelled like he was about to sandbagged by the New Yorkers.

Eventually most of the players came around. The Jersey contingent included Dan, Moyer, and Steve Nagiewicz, who crewed with Dan but also operated his own boat, the *Diversion*. Bielenda attended with one of his veteran *Wahoo* skippers, Janet Bieser, and Joel Silverstein, a close friend. Michael Emmerman also appeared. He was a veteran diver, New York City forensic investigator, and DAN board member.

In the all-day meeting, the dive boat captains explained their respective operations and practices. The sharpest contrast came when Dan and Bielenda outlined their opposing policies when it came to the certifications they required of their customers. Dan described the *Andrea Doria* as an almost an ideal wreck on which to train. Bielenda took exception and explained why he thought no one should be on the *Doria* who was not certified in the use of Trimix. Moyer sided with Bielenda.

Dan started to feel the meeting was a farce. He once again explained that he considered himself merely the "bus driver." He defended his reliance on the certification cards of the divers who paid to dive off the *Seeker*. He compared the cards to his own Coast Guard license, which allowed him to operate his vessel in coastal waters up to one hundred miles out to sea. The Coast Guard tested his knowledge and skills, then granted him the license. They assumed he knew what he was doing. It was the same with the divers. They came aboard with the certification cards. The cards were supposed to mean the divers had mastered the skills and knowledge represented by the certification program. Was he supposed to give the divers another test? He couldn't be expected to ask divers to physically demonstrate their diving skills before they were allowed aboard, could he? There was no way he could know every diver who walked down that dock at Star Island. Dan liked to say that he was not paid to baby-sit.

"It was a very serious discussion," said Mike Emmerman. "Dickerson wanted to know, was there any commonality to the accidents? Was there any one thing they could hang their hats on for these fatalities? So we analyzed all the incidents, one by one. No commonalities emerged at all from the discussion."

While a longtime Bielenda associate, Joel Silverstein does not consider himself a sworn enemy of Dan. He respects Dan as a diver and boat captain. Yet as he listened to the *Seeker* skipper speak, he remained mystified.

Silverstein had taught divers the fine points of Trimix use for a decade around the country. "It is a lot of work," he said. "You need controlled environments. You need environments where the diver has a safe haven. You can't do that when you're a hundred miles offshore. When a diver wants to go looking for things, artifacts, that's not when you should be working through your Trimix procedures. Ten or fifteen years ago, we trained on the [wreck] of the *Oregon,* or the *San Diego* [a sunken armored cruiser off Long Island]. You put in hundreds of dives on air. Then you tried Trimix. You worked on your craft. You refined your skills."

Silverstein grew concerned during the meeting. He made his livelihood in the technical-diving industry, and he did not want the Coast Guard to become overly involved. The candor at the meeting was remarkable but also potentially dangerous. He felt the Coast Guard had issued a "slightly veiled threat" to the boat captains that "if they didn't get their act together," their boats might be boarded by inspectors before they ever left for the *Andrea Doria.*

The meeting was tense. Dan's bus-driver speech remarks, as usual, rubbed some people the wrong way. With five people dead, and all of them from the *Seeker,* his remarks struck some as callous.

"You're not just a bus driver," Bielenda said. "You've got a responsibility."

"You run your boat your way," Dan fired back, "I'll run mine my way."

The uneasy summit in Coram ended with an agreement that those in attendance would contribute energy to a new "dive accident safety group." Dickerson saw to it that a list serve was arranged on the Internet. Maybe better communication was the answer.

But after three months, as the diving season once again approached, people stopped looking in on the list serve, or contributing messages to it, and it was disbanded.

"What bugs me the most is, this was needless," said Dickerson. It was February 2001, and he was explaining his new report on the death of Chris Murley. Dickerson was agitated by the Murley case. It bothered him more than the four other deaths at the *Andrea Doria* in 1998 and 1999. He felt that he didn't need to be an expert diver to know that inadequate measures were taken to safeguard Chris's life.

Dickerson started with what struck most people about Chris Murley: He was massive. In his report, Dickerson included the findings of a World Health Organization meeting on obesity in 1997. The unusual conference cited the numerous medical problems associated worldwide with excess weight. As a diagnostic tool for physicians, it recommended the establishment of a standardized Body Mass Index. The greater a person's BMI, the organization found, the greater the health risk.

WHO's experts calculated the BMI by dividing an individual's weight in kilograms (a kilogram is equivalent to 2.2 pounds) by the square of the person's height in meters (a meter equals 39.5 inches). They proposed three classes of obesity—Class I, Class II, and Class III, with Class III ranked the most serious. Anyone with a BMI over 30 was considered obese, and those with a BMI more than 40 were designated Class III obese. Chris listed himself on the Seeker data sheet as six foot eight, and 320 pounds. Translated into 145 kilograms and 2.02 meters, he had a BMI of 35. The medical examiner had weighed out Chris at 350; with that number, his BMI rose to 39.

"Chris Murley's final act," Dickerson wrote, "should not have been diving on the wreck of the *Andrea Doria*."

Dickerson also charged that Chris's instructor, Joe Jackson, had allowed Chris to dive even though he was aware that Chris had been diagnosed with diabetes. Dickerson was also convinced that Jackson had allowed Chris to dive because he and one other Cincinnati-based diver on the trip were in effect subsidizing the diving done by the *Seeker's* six-person crew for the trip and by Jackson himself.

"By letting Chris Murley go, Joe Jackson . . . received a free opportunity to dive on the *Andrea Doria* in addition to avoiding a monetary loss for the Cincinnati Dive Center," Dickerson wrote in his report.

He also could not understand why Murley, whose diving log showed less than ninety dives, with few of them in deep water—much less cold, deep water—had been allowed to dive.

Dickerson felt strongly about this point, though he was also aware that diving instructors worked under flexible standards that allowed them to ignore suggested minimum dive totals before recommending their students be certified.

The prerequisites of Technical Diving International's

Advanced Trimix course stated that an enrolled diver needed "a minimum of 100 logged dives or equivalent at the discretion of the instructor."

The leeway TDI allowed instructors such as Joe Jackson seemed logical given the organization's highly decentralized nature. In 1998, when Murley began his instruction with Jackson, TDI's training department employed seven people (four full time) to supervise and spot-check the activities of more than twenty-five hundred instructors all over the country. Two of those employees were usually confined to TDI's office in Topsham, Maine. The organization allowed its far-flung instructors to ignore the suggested minimum standards if, in their judgment, they deemed a student's abilities sufficient. Dickerson believed that Joe Jackson simply should not have exercised his discretion in the case of six-foot-eight, 320-pound Chris Murley.

"Chris Murley did not meet the prerequisites required by TDI to be taking the Advanced Trimix course, as he had not completed the minimum number of dives," Dickerson wrote. "In addition, based on his dive experience as logged, compared to other divers who have dove the *Andrea Doria*, it appears that he did not possess adequate deep diving experience to attempt this dive without a tremendous increase in risk." Dickerson sent copies of his report to all the agencies for which Jackson was a certified instructor—TDI; the National Association of Underwater Instructors (NAUI); and the biggest of all, the Professional Association of Diving Instructors (PADI).

Jackson and Dan sensed a looming shadow over their respective reputations. They were furious. "This report," Dan said, "is Dickerson's way of lashing back at both Joe and myself."

Jackson denied that Chris had ever told him he had diabetes—though Chris's fiancée, Mary Beth Byrne, contradicted him. "If I had known that, he wouldn't have dived," Jackson said. "Cut and dried—he would not have been in the water." He also bristled at the notion that he had allowed Chris to dive so he could get a free trip to the *Andrea Doria*. He stated that Chris Murley's charter had no particular financial impact on the Cincinnati Diving Center. The shop, Jackson said, had broken even on an earlier *Seeker* charter that summer, in which more divers were aboard.

Checking Chris's logbooks and a series of release forms on which Chris described his diving experience, Jackson said he was troubled that Chris had apparently exaggerated his diving history. The release form signed by Chris on April 8, 1999—three months before his death—contains blanks in which divers are to indicate for how long they have been diving and the total number of dives they have completed. Chris's form says he had been diving for one and a half years and had logged 130 dives. Neither statement is true. In April 1999, Chris had been diving for just fourteen months and had logged just seventy dives.

Jackson's surprise was, however, baffling. He had accompanied Chris on the Pompano Beach training trip in late June, with Chris's final dive of the trip taking place on June 20. That dive, on the shipwrecked *RB Johnson*, had marked Chris's eighty-first dive. Did Jackson assume that Chris had somehow logged forty-nine dives between June 20 and the day he died, July 21? If nothing else, Jackson's presentation of himself as an instructor who worked closely with his students, who guided their individual ascents through ever-more-complicated levels of training, appeared to have been profoundly undermined.

Dan defended his position with confidence. He had worked many times with Joe Jackson and had come to rely on Jackson's judgment about the divers he brought from Cincinnati. Dan relied on people such as Joe Jackson, he said, because there were too many divers from too many places for him to track. Dickerson had recommended the *Seeker* crew check the precise experience level of each diver who stepped aboard. "It's like Dickerson is telling me I have to check out every little detail about every single person on my boat," Dan said. "That's why you have release forms."

The *Seeker*'s release form was then two pages long. Each of its fifteen paragraphs had a space for the signatory to initial. One paragraph allowed Dan and Jenn's company, Deep Explorers, Inc., "to use, in whole or in part" the signee's "name likeness, image, voice, biography, interview, and performance in connection with the *Seeker*."

The form also compelled the diver who signed it to give up his or her right to sue Deep Explorers, along with the International Association of Nitrox and Technical Divers, Technical Divers International, or the TDI division known as Scuba Diving International, or SDI.

The form also required divers to avow that they were physically fit and that they assumed the risk in scuba diving. It plainly described the sport as "ultra-hazardous" when conducted below 130 feet. Finally, Dan's form made it clear that divers who stepped aboard the *Seeker* were ultimately on their own.

"I understand that I have a duty to plan and carry out my own dive and to be responsible for my own safety and should I elect to dive with a buddy, it is to be an arrangement solely between that buddy and myself," read the paragraphs initialed by Chris. "Deep Explorers, Inc., IANTD, TDI/SDI, and their officers, agents, servants, and/or employees are not responsible for providing me with a diving partner or in any way coordination [*sic*] my dive with another diver."

Chris initialed every blank on the release form, indicating to others that he apparently knew what he was getting into.

As he listened on the telephone, Richard Lefkowitz could look around his law office and see a photograph of himself a decade earlier, on the deck of a charter dive boat above the wreck of the *Andrea Doria*.

In the photograph, Lefkowitz held a ceramic vase he had retrieved from the ship, its surface greasy with the brown muck of the wreck site. His shoulders were beefy, and his smile was wide, white, with a couple of large teeth up front and slightly spaced. His face and arms were brown from hours of threading his high-performance fiberglass kayak through the canals and channels of the South Shore of Long Island. On a bookshelf, Lefkowitz kept a cup and plate he had plucked from the *Doria*. Both bore the blue-and-gold stripes that graced all of the liner's second-class china. Next to this was the same vase as in the photo on the wall, cleaned up now, its buttercup glaze aglow.

Outside, traffic crawled along Old Country Road and whisked by on nearby Meadowbrook Parkway. Lefkowitz's office was in one of Long Island's most recognizable office buildings, not least because of its street address, 666. The nine-story building was an island in the sprawling ocean of the island's low-slung suburban sprawl. Like ranks of schooled fish, two lanes of cars turned continually into the black lots surrounding Long Island's largest indoor mall, Roosevelt Field Shopping Center. Here, on a cloudy day seventy-two years earlier, aviator Charles Lindbergh had taken off for France. Long Islanders had little interest in preserving this historic spot, however, and the great mall rose, though Lindbergh's contribution to the history of flight was honored with a plaque inside, under a staircase and across from the Disney Store.

Lefkowitz leaned back in his chair and listened to the caller. It was Steve Bielenda, operator of the *Wahoo*. Bielenda had spoken with Mark Kammer, a close friend of Chris Murley, and Bielenda told Lefkowitz that Murley's elderly parents were considering filing a lawsuit against the *Seeker*, TDI, Deep Explorers, Inc., Dan, and Jenn.

Lefkowitz had made his handful of dives on the *Doria* from Bielenda's boat. A poster-sized photo of the *Wahoo* speeding along in the Atlantic leaned against the office bookshelf. Lefkowitz had once represented Bielenda in a case in which a member of the *Wahoo*'s crew was injured by the boat's propeller. In the New York–New Jersey cultural divide that grouped divers in the metropolitan area, Lefkowitz was a New York guy firmly in the *Wahoo* camp.

He couldn't believe what he was hearing.

He had never heard of Chris Murley, and he could not understand why the man was even at the *Andrea Doria*, much less diving on it, much less on Trimix. Lefkowitz had cut back on his diving in the past few years, but he remained well acquainted with the typical career arc of most divers in the region.

First, they might dive on the USS *San Diego*, the armored cruiser that wrecked in 110 feet of water after apparently striking a German mine in 1918; then on the Cunard liner *Oregon*, sunk in 1886 in 130 feet of water after colliding with another ship; then on the *Sommerstad* (or *Virginia*, as the locals called it), sunk to the depth of 180 feet after taking one of the Kaiser's torpedoes amidships in 1918; then on the oil tanker *Coimbra*, sunk in 1942, yet another victim of the German navy, and also at about 180 feet. Those shipwrecks, in that order, represented a common progression in Northeast wreck diving. All could be reached in an afternoon's ride from either the South Shore of Long Island or the Jersey shore, which was the opposite landfall in the section of the Atlantic known as the New York Bight. A diver who ping-ponged back and forth for years amid these challenging dive sites might then eventually give the *Andrea Doria* a try.

Chris Murley had made none of these dives. He had never made a dive in cold water with hard current. His ocean experience was largely limited to the trip to Florida, where his fumbling dives in warm water were met with concern and criticism by Joe Jackson.

Lefkowitz felt that someone should be held accountable for the fate of Chris Murley. At the same time, he recognized that the legal obstacles to establishing negligence would be substantial. Chris had signed many releases along the way that had sought to release from liability just about everyone involved in his becoming a diver and in taking him to the *Andrea Doria*. Lefkowitz knew about such releases because he had signed them himself many times when he boarded diving charter boats. Unless the releases were fraudulent, defective, or invalid, Lefkowitz knew he faced high odds against success.

He took the case anyway. He would take one-third of any award, but on contingency. The plaintiffs—Chris Murley's father, William Murley, and Mary Beth Byrne—could hardly afford to pay him by the hour as he built the case and flew around taking depositions. The case could trigger a big payoff or it could be a series of legal maneuvers so doomed from the start that on paper the action would seem almost pointless.

Lefkowitz wasn't a personal admirer of Chris Murley. He was incredulous about Chris's fixation about the Italian Line's bathroom fixtures. He did not understand why someone so new to deep diving would break at least two of the sport's fundamental rules—to plan each dive with care and not to become overly goal oriented. Chris also seemed in denial about his basic lack of physical conditioning. It seemed possible he had also shaded the truth in speaking to others about his diabetes. Lefkowitz couldn't be sure.

And yet, Lefkowitz also believed, Chris had not been served properly by the diving industry. He had been encouraged in his self-delusion by a certification system and charter boat that, in their collective priorities, had apparently ranked Chris's safety below their concerns about revenue flow. If he did not take the case, Lefkowitz thought, who would?

Although nine years had passed since his last dive on the *Andrea Doria*, Lefkowitz's memories of his own descent to the wreck contributed to his decision to take the Murley case. He was not a diver on the order of, say, Gary Gentile—far, far from it—but he knew the *Andrea Doria*. He had planted his feet on the wreck's hull, so overgrown with marine life that it seemed like the seafloor itself. He had shared the exciting but unsettling surge in adrenaline of others who landed on the ship and who suddenly felt, in one intoxicating jolt, as if they had shrunk to the size of toy soldiers.

Rich Lefkowitz recalled his moments on the *Andrea Doria* as a magnificent experience. He had bagged a fat, muddy load of china and had returned safely. He kept the china within his view every day of his working life. He eventually pulled back from the endless weekends of wreck diving to focus more on his career and his family.

He knew the wreck, he knew what it took to get there, and he was convinced Chris Murley should never have been there at all.

Twelve

By June 11, 2002, when he sat down in a conference room at the Four Points Sheraton hotel in Cincinnati to give a deposition in Richard Lefkowitz's lawsuit, Joe Jackson no longer worked as an instructor at the Cincinnati Diving Center.

He had left the shop about fifteen months after the death of his student Chris Murley. He was a self-employed scuba instructor after having worked for one year putting together a market survey for Diving Unlimited International, an equipment manufacturer. As a result of Chris's death, Jackson's certification as an instructor had been briefly suspended by the diving agencies whose programs he taught. But they quickly cleared him of any wrongdoing. He worked freelance, sometimes flown in to lead a group of diving students through a certification course.

Lefkowitz had sued for thirty-five million dollars. The action, brought in federal court on behalf of Chris's parents and his fiancée, Mary Beth Byrne, argued that Chris's death was due to negligence on the part of Dan, Jennifer Samulski, Technical Diving International, the Cincinnati Diving Center and its owner Steven Bernstein, and diving center instructors Rick Vanover and Joe Jackson.

The lawsuit noted that Chris had begun recreational diving in February 1998 and that at the time of his death, in July of the following year, he was working on his sixth diving certification. Sometimes, to speed his progress toward his goal of diving the *Doria* and removing a toilet for the room he envisioned in his home, Chris took courses concurrently. His principal instructor in all six courses had been Joe Jackson.

Among the many allegations in the suit were that the defendants had been reckless in permitting Chris "to attempt dives to the *Andrea Doria*, with knowledge of the fact that he had failed to demonstrate the diving skills necessary to obtain his Trimix Certification only weeks before." This charge referred to Chris's flawed execution of Trimix techniques during his trip to deep-water dive sites in Florida with Jackson.

For their part, the defendants relied heavily on the chain of liability releases that Chris Murley had signed—one each time he entered a new class at the Cincinnati Diving Center. He had signed forms stating that he knew technical diving was inherently dangerous, that he assumed the risk involved, and that his instructors and certification agency would not be held liable if he were injured or killed. Carefully crafted and standard across the industry, the releases were extremely effective against litigators such as Rich Lefkowitz.

To have any hope of getting the case before a jury, Lefkowitz needed to prove his contention in the lawsuit that the defendants had been reckless in "accepting [Chris] into the Trimix training course with knowledge of the fact that he did not possess the minimum training and/or experience required for admission." He had little hope of making the case, however, if he could not prove that the release forms were somehow fraudulent.

Rich Lefkowitz liked to tell a story about a time he went to Key West on a vacation and went into a local dive shop there. He planned to dive on some local deep shipwrecks and wanted to rent equipment. The proprietor asked him to produce a dive log, just to make sure that the fast-talking visitor from New York knew what he was doing. The dive shop's healthy skepticism left a deep impression on Lefkowitz. In his opinion, Chris Murley should have aroused the same sort of questioning attitude from Jackson and the crew of the *Seeker*.

To chip away at the release forms, Lefkowitz initially would rely on two key documents. The first was a syllabus for TDI's Advanced Trimix Diver Course, which listed as prerequisites other certifications and a "minimum of 100 logged dives or equivalent at the discretion of the instructor."

The second document was the TDI general liability release, dated April 8, 1999. On this, Chris had untruthfully stated he had been diving for one and a half years and had executed 130 dives.

Because Joe Jackson's signature appeared throughout Chris's comprehensive log of his dives—a log that listed just eighty-nine dives—Lefkowitz was incredulous that Jackson would sign off on Chris's claim that he had made 130 dives. If Jackson were truly that gullible—and Lefkowitz judged him far from naive—it seemed at odds with Jackson's description of himself. Was he not a subtle handler of personalities who routinely aborted dives with students if he sensed even that their "body posture" indicated unease?

Jackson's willingness to believe that Chris had the required number of dives seemed doubly strange to Lefkowitz because Chris had fouled up the Florida training dives just a couple of weeks before the expedition to the *Andrea Doria*. It did not seem plausible that Jackson believed Chris had made 130 dives, much less 100.

"You stated," Lefkowitz said in the hotel conference room in Cincinnati, "that Mr. Murley was a student of yours on almost a continuous basis from February of '98 through the time that he took his Trimix training—"

"Yes," Jackson replied.

"—and the time you took this form [the TDI release] to him?"

"Yes."

"And did you dive with him frequently?"

"Quite a bit."

"Did you have any independent knowledge of the number of dives that he completed?"

"No," said Jackson.

"Did you check his logbook at the time that you accepted this form from him . . . to clarify that the information was accurate?"

"I'm sorry. What?"

"Did you check the logbook so as to check the dives?"

"No, I didn't."

"You did not check his logbook?"

"No, because he put down that he had 130 dives on the form. I had no reason to not believe him. I thought he was an honest person."

Later in the deposition, Jackson explained why he had not issued Chris his certification card for Trimix diving. He felt that Chris, in Florida in the third week of June, had not demonstrated he had learned all the required skills or could exercise the mature judgment necessary to make such dives. When Chris went to the *Andrea Doria*, he had eleven Trimix dives to his credit. Jackson thought he needed more.

"Is there a reason why you had not issued that certification prior to departing for the *Andrea Doria*?" Lefkowitz asked.

"Yes," Jackson said.

"And can you tell me the reason, please?"

"Yes. I have a responsibility for their safety, and Chris had told me he had every intention of penetrating the wreck and if I didn't take him he'd just go with somebody else. And for that reason I couldn't just give him a card, because some other boat, if I couldn't talk to them first, would let him on board and he could get himself in trouble.

"So I told him the first trip he went up there he was going to have to go with me and he would have to dive with me, and if he did everything okay, then I would issue his card. But it was to hold him back from doing something that may get him hurt."

"Okay," said Lefkowitz, "and the purpose in diving with him on the trips to the *Andrea Doria* was to prevent him from penetrating into the wreck?"

"Keep him from penetrating the wreck," Jackson said. "And I liked Chris, I didn't mind giving up my normal dives to dive with him, and it was fun to see him so excited, seeing him doing something he had dreamed of."

Sometimes when Denis Murphy heard a stock market report on the radio, he thought of Vince Napoliello. Vince had worked on Wall Street, and the two men had talked a lot about money. Murphy planned to make some investments with Vince's professional guidance.

The stock market reports were a mental trigger for Murphy. He saw the dive on the *Andrea Doria* from three years earlier.

He felt the regulator being ripped out his mouth, saw the burst of bubbles from the free-flow. Then he was holding Vince by the equipment harness and screaming, "You all right?" Vince once again returned that weird, blank stare. What did it mean? Then they hurried out of the ship, they separated, Murphy hunkered down on the deck, prepared to ascend. Finally, Vince swam away and vanished.

Murphy felt he should never have let go of Vince. He should have stayed with Vince. Maybe they could have figured out the problem together. They had buddied up on the dive, after all. Things might have turned out differently.

While Murphy second-guessed his decision to split away from Vince, no one else associated with the *Seeker* did so. They all felt they had moved beyond the buddy system that was so integral to scuba diving that took place in shallower waters. Craig Sicola had dived alone, and Richard Roost had dived alone. Charlie McGurr dived with a team but separated from it. *Seeker* divers felt that there probably wasn't much you could do to help a diver in serious trouble at 250 feet anyway. They all said they knew the risks.

People associated with the Vince Napoliello incident had largely moved forward in their lives by the summer of 2002. Bill Cleary, the lawyer who had organized the charter, had purchased his own boat and was ferrying divers to local wrecks. Marisa Gengaro, Vince's fiancée, had met another man and had married him. Murphy pulled back from deep diving for a while and focused on his young son.

Still, when he heard a stock report, or even when he sat down and read about investing, the memories unspooled.

Regulator, bubbles, swimming, separation, then Vince slowly disappears, like a climber ascending into a cloud. The memories, he told people, were his "little demons," and he wanted to exorcise them by returning to the wreck of the *Andrea Doria*.

He drove from northern New Jersey out to Montauk and arrived at the Star Island Marina on July 23. But the weather boiled offshore. Dan canceled the charter. As Murphy drove back to New Jersey, he told himself he would return to the *Doria* the next year.

Since Vince's death, Murphy had made another decision about his scuba diving. He would no longer dive with a partner. He did not want to feel responsible for anything that might happen to anyone else. He planned to explore the *Doria* alone.

All he wanted was what he called a "clean dive" on the wreck. He didn't care if he bagged any china. He had china. All he desired was to dive safely on the *Andrea Doria* and return home alive.

Then, Murphy decided, he would never go back again.

A month later, it was Dan's turn to testify under oath in a deposition. Rich Lefkowitz had driven over from Long Island down to Eatontown, New Jersey, just north of Brick, where Dan and Jenn lived.

Dan had been underwater diving when Chris Murley had been stricken on the surface, so Lefkowitz would not center his questions on how exactly Chris had died. Chris had drowned, according to the medical examiner's report, which suggested that his face must have dipped below the water's surface when he was still alive. But Lefkowitz wasn't confident he could ever determine what exactly happened when Chris was in the water. All the witnesses to those events were, at least in theory, hostile to him. Instead, he focused instead on why Chris was in the water in the first place.

Lefkowitz was interested in the extent to which Dan monitored the divers who came aboard the *Seeker* to dive on the *Doria*.

Dan explained that, before departure for *Andrea Doria* trips, the divers were required to submit signed liability releases, photocopies of their health insurance cards, and documentation that showed they either were certified in the proper use of Trimix or would be diving with their Trimix instructor.

"And then there came a time that the boat did depart Montauk for a scheduled *Andrea Doria* charter?" Lefkowitz said.

"Yes," said Dan.

"And Mr. Murley was a member of that party?"

"Yes."

"Did you have any conversation with Mr. Murley at any time prior to departing dock?"

"I would imagine I have a conversation with just about everybody."

"And do you recall any of those conversations?"

"Not directly."

"Who on your boat was responsible to determine that the divers on this trip met your particulars or qualifications?" asked Lefkowitz.

"Mr. Jackson," said Dan, "since it was his charter."

"Does the boat—did anyone on the boat make any inquiry to determine if Mr. Jackson's charter passengers had met the necessary requirements?"

"Yes. Our requirements, yes. Our minimum requirements, yes. Myself or Miss Samulski."

"Did you make any inquiry of Mr. Jackson, or did you review any of the paperwork sent by Mr. Jackson to show that the members of this trip met your minimum requirements?"

"I'm sure I probably did.,"

"Do you have any recollection of having done so?"

"No."

As he did earlier in the summer with Joe Jackson, Lefkowitz then focused on two documents. First was a *Seeker* "Diver Data Sheet" filled out by Chris. Dan and Jenn asked their divers to complete the one-page form, which provided contact numbers, medical information, and certification status.

In Chris's case, the court had received from the *Seeker* a copy of the data sheet. The boat had sent the original of the sheet with Chris when he was airlifted by the Coast Guard. Jenn had then copied the original information to a new data sheet, Dan testified.

"And this is an exact duplicate as far as you understand of the information contained?" Lefkowitz asked.

"Yes," Dan said. "This is a handwritten copy of that information that was on the original."

"Did you review the original before the time that you took this charter out to sea?"

"Yes."

And did you review Mr. Murley's original?"

"Yes."

The original, however, was not the same as the copy. Lefkowitz had received the original when the Coast Guard's file on the case was forwarded to his office. On the original Diver Data Sheet, where the form asked for certification level, Chris had written "Nitrox"—a mixed-gas certification one level below Trimix.

When Jennifer made the new form, she had written "Nitrox" then had penciled in what to Lefkowitz seemed a convenient upgrade: "Adv Trimix Pending."

Jenn's editing squared with her understanding of Chris's status. He was in training. But Lefkowitz suspected that Jenn's apparent addendum to the form suggested a pattern of shading the truth about Chris Murley's qualifications to dive on the wreck. He wondered whether Jackson and the *Seeker* owners made an effort to match Chris's qualifications with those demanded by the *Seeker.* Lefkowitz did not push these questions at the depositions, however. He decided the point might be better withheld and used later as ammunition against what he expected would be a exceptionally strong effort by the defendants' attorneys to have the case dismissed based on the liability releases.

Lefkowitz's second important document was a "Diver Registration Form" issued by TDI. Joe Jackson had apparently filled out the form on June 20 in anticipation of getting a certification card for Chris. The "Course Location" listed was Pompano Beach, Florida, where Chris had demonstrated he had a few skills to hone before Jackson would issue him the certification.

On July 1, sometime after he notified Chris he had decided he could go to the *Andrea Doria,* Jackson signed the form. He did not send it in to TDI's office in Maine to get the certification card, however. He had told Chris that he could probably get the card if he performed well at the *Doria.* He faxed the form to Dan and Jenn.

Dan was familiar with such forms because he was also a
Trimix instructor for TDI. The form had been signed by Joe
Jackson above a paragraph that said, "I certify that the above
named students have completed the TDI training course indicat-
ed and have reached the proficiency level required by TDI
Standards before issuing these certifications."

Dan, however, drew a larger meaning from the form. He said
the form indicated to him that the diver involved was either a
student or "when he gets his card, he'll be certified."

Lefkowitz was perplexed. The form said nothing about being
under instruction.

"But the signature on the bottom of that page would tell
you that he was certified, would it not?" he asked.

"I would think so," Dan agreed.

Lefkowitz began to feel that he would be able to make the
case before a judge that Dan had apparently relied on a document that he claimed said Chris was a Trimix student about to
be certified when that document said no such thing. Lefkowitz
might argue that such an action by Dan was negligent. Now
Lefkowitz wanted to establish how closely the bus driver looked
after the people who had climbed aboard. Especially a passenger
who had died.

"Now, is this a form Mr. Jackson gave you before or after the
charter?" he asked

"I couldn't tell you, but I would think it would be before,"
Dan replied.

"Did you review Mr. Murley's logbook before boarding?"

"No."

"Did you question Mr. Murley as to the number of dives he

completed and where he may have completed those dives prior to coming on your vessel?"

"No."

"Did anyone do that on your behalf?"

"No."

"Do you review requirements or do you review the credentials of divers before they would board your boat to dive a wreck such as the *Andrea Doria*?"

"No."

"Does anyone do that on your behalf?"

"No."

Not long before he had given the deposition, Dan had wrapped up the diving season on the *Andrea Doria*. Whereas during 1998 and 1999, he had scheduled as many as eleven charters for the great wreck, that summer of 2002 he offered just three.

Dan's business fortunes reflected disappointing industry trends. The American economy had cooled since the late 1990s, and the terrorist attacks in New York and Washington on September 11, 2001, had further added to the chill. Compared to five years previously, extreme sports such as scuba diving were not drawing the same numbers of people. The segment of divers who rushed into the sport for only one reason—to lay claim to china from the *Andrea Doria*—apparently had been weeded out.

The divers who had raked over the artifacts at the *Doria* through the 1990s also were now a few years older, and deep diving took on new physical risks. So a few more backed away from the sport. People in their midforties and fifties simply could not do as much deep diving as people in their thirties

("I'm in a situation where I'm working off the backside of the baby boom," Dan said). It was not clear now that the Northeast's dive boats would ever serve as many customers as they had in the 1980s and 1990s.

And, at least to some in the Northeast wreck-diving community, the *Seeker* was no longer the hot ride to the *Andrea Doria*.

Few inside the industry doubted Dan's ability as a boat captain or even as a safe operator of dive charters. But the overall *Seeker* act had apparently worn a bit thin. With money a little tighter, and everyone aging, divers were not as willing as they'd once been to spend a weekend on the fringes of the hypercritical clique of big boys. "Divers, when they rise up to the level of these expedition-type dives, such as the *Andrea Doria*, they all have a pretty good sense of who they feel comfortable with and who they are impressed with," said Gene Peterson, owner of Atlantic Divers, the southern New Jersey shop that took Craig Sicola to the wreck in 1998. "People who say they are the only dive boat to go out on, well, that starts to become a little too much for some people."

Dan didn't seem to mind.

He never tried to please everyone. He sensed that a very few people steered away from the *Seeker* because of the fatalities of 1998 and 1999, but his conscience remained clear. He would always be a little bit angry with Craig Sicola, whom he felt was a much better diver than he had demonstrated on the wreck. Otherwise, he felt his boat had simply endured a nasty run of bad luck. The deaths, he maintained, simply reflected the fact that his boat for a few years had taken more people to the wreck than anyone else. It was a numbers game, and he had lost. "Nobody out there had any kind of problem as far as their diving was concerned," he said. "No one died because they didn't have the proper training. People died due to unknown medical conditions. The way I look at it, everybody basically succumbed to circumstances."

With fewer customers for the charter work, Dan had gone back to commercial diving five days a week. He spent part of the fall of 2002 working underwater at Battery Park City, where he and other unionized workers were helping with a pier maintenance project. Hour after hour, they hammered together concrete forms, then pumped in the concrete. Dan's underwater film work had slowed down, in part because his favorite outlets for the work, places such as the History Channel and the Discovery Channel, had reduced their budgets for new productions. Even so, he had found a quirky project he believed in, and enjoyed: Ever the entrepreneur, he had started looking around for people related to passengers and crew members who had been lost on some of the better-known shipwrecks in New York and New Jersey, and he had begun conducting interviews on camera. A lot of the people he interviewed had no idea what had happened to their relative, or how the ship was lost. Maybe he had something there.

A few of the usual requests, meanwhile, stacked up at Dan and Jenn's home. People wanted to know if he would take them out to the wreck of the *Andrea Doria*. A whole group of Canadian divers sent in a request. Dan decided to wait and see how many such requests stacked up. For now, it was a pile of letters.

For the first time in a decade, Dan, now forty-two years old, had no interest in the idea of diving on the wreck of the *Andrea*

Doria. The cost of docking the *Seeker* at Montauk was steep, and he did not burn for another dive to the wreck. For him, operating the *Seeker* had always been about the diving. He wasn't comfortable with all the charter paperwork; Jenn handled that. He also didn't see himself as a career scuba instructor. He could teach, but it wasn't his passion. Once, during a Trimix class at his home, he flipped through the course book in front of the class and said, "I really don't care about a lot of this shit if you can save your ass when the shit hits the fan."

He was a diver. He liked to dive with the best. And the *Seeker* had been his vehicle to the most challenging, most fascinating shipwreck dives in the region.

Now the best dive of them all, the *Andrea Doria*, had undergone a dramatic transformation. In the previous couple of seasons, the entire Promenade Deck, the level where people had stacked their luggage almost fifty years earlier in anticipation of arrival in New York, had sheared off and avalanched to the seafloor.

Something elemental about the wreck had been lost. The mountain was smaller. It was less spectacular. This was no longer a staggeringly beautiful ocean liner that had come to rest almost graciously on its side. Now it was so much unrecognizable till. There were piles of tortured steel bulkheads, and mystery girders, and wires leading nowhere.

Now, Dan said, the wreck of the *Andrea Doria* was a pile of junk. He didn't want to be the "master" of a pile of junk. He was certain that the wreck would continue to draw divers, especially because the collapse of the Promenade Deck had exposed new chinks where the ship's china would surely be found.

"For those who are looking strictly for artifacts, they are chomping at the bit," he said. "It could be easy pickings."

But Dan was not chomping at the bit anymore.

He had decided that he had more china from the wreck of *Andrea Doria* than he knew what to do with.

Afterword

Depositions in the Chris Murley case continued in 2002, and attorneys' motions thickened the legal file through most of 2003, but in the end, Dan Crowell prevailed.

On August 27, 2003, U.S. District Court Judge Arthur D. Spatt dismissed the lawsuit filed by Murley's estate against Dan, Jenn, Joe Jackson, Steve Bernstein, the Cincinnati Diving Center, and Technical Diving International. Although the depositions had centered on whether Chris had been competent at the Andrea Doria, or whether Joe Jackson had correctly cleared Chris for the dives, little of that mattered to Judge Spatt. He focused on the three liability releases that Chris had signed holding his instructors and the Seeker charter harmless. Chris had willingly signed them. It was immaterial that he appeared to have lied on them, or that others apparently were aware of the lies.

Dan said he had felt "vilified" in the press over the suit. Now he felt vindicated.

"We had no doubts about the outcome," he told me after Spatt issued his ruling. "The whole thing was ridiculous."

I asked him if he would change anything about how he operated the Seeker during the Murley trip. "Nothing whatsoever."

Dan did not return to the Andrea Doria in the summer of 2003. He took his customers to other shipwrecks, and he poured energy into a film about the USS *Murphy*, a World War II destroyer that sank about 80 miles from the Jersey shore. He had been tracking down survivors of the sinking and interviewing them on videotape. A few other dive boats visited the Andrea Doria wreck site, but they did not take nearly as many people as the Seeker had in its heydey. One diver from New Jersey, diving from a Staten Island-based boat, had died while diving the Doria in 2002. The boat's captain, Joseph Terzuoli, said William Schmoldt, 54, had for some unknown reason "free-ascended," causing catastrophic lung injuries. Schmoldt had been conscious and talking when dragged from the water, but died undergoing treatment in a hyperbaric oxygen chamber at a hospital in North Providence, R.I. Doctors were able to revive Schmoldt twice when he suffered two heart attacks in the chamber. When he suffered a third attack, he died.

Nevertheless, Dan continued to be identified with the Andrea Doria. At diving shows, where he once again was billed as the Andrea Doria's "master," Dan was among those who agreed that he bore little responsibility for what had happened to his customers who never returned from the wreck. Dan told me Chris Murley had "known full-well" what he was getting into at the wreck. And an experienced federal judge had agreed. "The decedent had enough experience to understand the dangers of scuba diving and clearly accepted the risks," wrote Spatt.

Spatt's ruling also noted, however, that the defendants—Dan, Jenn, Joe Jackson, and TDI—"concede that Murley made less than 100 dives." In other words, they conceded that Chris had not made enough dives to receive the Adanced Trimix Diver certification Joe Jackson had awarded to him. But Chris had penned his initials next to every paragraph of the carefully drafted releases, which are standard through the industry. "While Murley may have lacked the physical stamina and training for such an advanced dive, there is no showing that Murley signed all three releases unwittingly," the judge wrote.

As Bart Malone liked to say, it's "big boy diving" at the wreck of the Andrea Doria. It was difficult for those associated with the Seeker to imagine that anyone would stretch the truth when it came to diving the Doria, at least in a way that would risk their physical safety. No one on the Seeker was prepared, or even especially interested in, protecting a guy such as Chris Murley from his worst impulses. That's not the way it works with big boys.

Every course handbook, they pointed out, states that certifications were always granted, ultimately, at the discretion of the instructor. If the student fell a few dives short, the instructor could still award the certification if he or she judged the student prepared.

"This whole experience-level thing," Dan said, "there is no set, specific number of dives for this certification or that certification. Everything falls back to the student. With the certifications, you've passed a test. That's really all it is."

"Not for nothing, but it call comes back to the old saying: 'I'm just a bus driver.'"

As Dan made his point, I could not help recalling that cold winter day I spent in the basement at his tidy Brick, N.J. home, where he was leading a group through the "classroom" portion of a technical diving certification. I had to go back to my notebook to capture the old quotation correctly. He had flipped through the thick diving text and said, "I really don't care about a lot of this shit if you can save your own ass when the shit hits the fan."

Others were moving on, too. Kathleen McGurr, widow of Charlie McGurr, who had sued Dan over her husband's death, had settled the case for $5,000, Dan said. Marisa Gengaro, who had been engaged to Vince Napoliello, found a new love, married and lives in New Jersey. She said she would never forget Vince, but that she was truly happy in her new life.

One day a card postmarked "Pompton Plains, N.J.," arrived in the mail at my home on Long Island. It was a note from Vince's mother. She told me she wished I could have met her son. She said he was a careful man and a good and decent son.

She said she thought of Vince every day.

—J. H.
FEBRUARY 2004
BAY SHORE, NEW YORK

Selected Sources

NEWSPAPERS

Asbury Park Press, Bergen (N.J.) *Record, Boston Herald, Cape Cod Times, Cincinnati Post, Detroit News, News and Observer* (Raleigh, N.C.), *New Haven Register, New York Times, Newsday, Patriot Ledger, Philadelphia Inquirer, The Sandpaper* (N.J.).

BOOKS

Bachrach, Arthur J. and Egstrom, Glen H. *Stress and Performance in Diving.* San Pedro, Calif.: Best Publishing Co., 1987.

Ballard, Robert D. and Archbold, Rick. *Lost Liners: From the* Titanic *to the* Andrea Doria, *The Ocean Floor Reveals Its Greatest Lost Ships.* New York: Hyperion, 1997.

Berg, Daniel. *Wreck Valley, Vol. II: A Record of Shipwrecks Off Long Island's South Shore and New Jersey.* East Rockaway, NY: Aqua Explorers, Inc, 1990.

Bookspan, Jolie. *Diving Physiology in Plain English.* Kensington, Maryland: Undersea and Hyperbaric Medical Society, 1997.

Carson, Rachel. *The Sea Around Us.* New York: Oxford University Press, 1950

Chowdhury, Bernie. *The Last Dive.* New York: Perennial, 2000.

Ecott, Tim. *Neutral Buoyancy: Adventures in a Liquid World.* New York: Atlantic Monthly Press, 2001.

Gentile, Gary. Andrea Doria: *Dive to an Era.* Philadelphia: Gary Gentile Productions, 1989.

Goldstein, Richard. *Desperate Hours: The Epic Rescue of the* Andrea Doria. New York: John Wiley & Sons, Inc., 2001.

Hoffer, William. *Saved! The Story of the* Andrea Doria—*The Greatest Sea Rescue in History.* New York: Summit Books, 1979.

Keatts, Henry C. *New York & New Jersey: Guide to Shipwreck Diving.* Houston: Pisces Books, 1992.

McMurray, Kevin F. *Deep Descent: Adventure and Death Diving the* Andrea Doria. New York: Pocket Books, 2001.

Moscow, Alvin. *Collision Course: The* Andrea Doria *and the* Stockholm. New York: G.P. Putnam's Sons, 1959.

Mountain, Alan. *The Diver's Handbook.* first published in London by New Holland Publishers, Ltd., 1996. Subsequently published in New York by The Lyons Press, 1997.

Phillips, John L. *The Bends: Compressed Air in the History of Science, Diving and Engineering.* New Haven, Conn.: Yale University Press, 1998.

ARTICLES

Carrothers, John C. "A Case for the Department of Justic. The *Andrea Doria–Stockholm* Collision. Unpublished manuscript. 1985.

Carrothers, John C. "The *Andrea Doria–Stockholm* Disaster: Accidents Don't Happen." U.S. Naval Institute *Proceedings,* August 1971.

Chatterton, John. "Searching for Shipwrecks." *Immersed,* Spring 1996.

Chenney, Timothy L. and Lassen, Lorenz. "Recreational Scuba Diving Injuries." *American Family Physician,* April 1996.

Hunt, Jennifer C. "Divers' Accounts of Normal Risk." *Symbolic Interaction,* Vol. 18, Number 4, 1995.

Hunt, Jennifer C. "Psychological Aspects of Scuba Diving Injuries: Suggestions for Short-Term Treatment from a Psychodynamic Perspective." *Journal of Clinical Psychology in Medical Settings,* Vol. 13, Number 3, 1996.

Keatts, Henry. "*Andrea Doria:* An Unlikely Tragedy." *Discover Diving,* April, 1997.

Lander, Barb. "Diving the *Doria:* It's Definitely Not for Everyone." *Sport Diver,* March/April 1996.

Lord, Walter. "Amid Terror on the Sinking 'Doria:' An Epic Sea Rescue." *Life,* Aug. 6, 1956.

MacLeish, Kenneth. "Divers Explore the Sunken 'Doria.'" *Life,* Sept. 17, 1956.

"Medical Problems of Recreational Scuba Diving." *American Family Physician,* June 1, 2001.

McMahon, Bucky. "Everest at the Bottom of the Sea." *Esquire,* July 2000.

McMurray, Kevin F. "Deep Secrets." *Yankee,* July 1999.

Saphire, William B. "The Rebirth of Italy's Merchant Marine," *Ships and the Sea,* January 1954.

"Technical Data on the SS *Andrea Doria.*" *The Travel Agent,* Jan. 25, 1953.

WEBSITES

Grillo, Anthony. www.andreadoria.org.